British Sports Cars

RICHARD GUNN

CLASSIC VEHICLES SERIES, VOLUME 5

Picture credits: Aston Martin, Bentley Drivers' Club, Bentley Motors, Brooklands Museum, Ford Motor Company, Goodwood Road Racing Company, Jaguar Land Rover, James Peene, Lotus Cars, Magic Car Pics, McLaren Automotive, Mercedes-Benz, Morgan Motor Company, Public Domain, Richard Gunn, RM Sotherby's, Sunbeam Lotus Owners' Club, Russ Smith, Theo Ford-Sagers, Ultima Sports Ltd, Vauxhall Motors, Wikimedia Commons.

Published by Key Books
An imprint of Key Publishing Ltd
PO Box 100
Stamford
Lincs PE19 1XQ

www.keypublishing.com

The right of Richard Gunn to be identified as the author of this book has been asserted in accordance with the Copyright, Designs and Patents Act 1988 Sections 77 and 78.

Copyright © Richard Gunn, 2021

ISBN 978 1 80282 039 3

Typeset by SJmagic DESIGN SERVICES, India.

Contents

Chapter 1

Pioneering Days

After centuries of being limited to the speed of a galloping horse, the industrial revolution started to open new transport opportunities. But it took the invention of the internal combustion engine to really open up new horizons.

By the standards of the time, any of the first automobiles could be classed as sports cars, simply because they offered personal speed unlike anything else before. The 19th Century was ruled by the steam engine and the horse, but for the vast majority of the British population, walking or cycling would have been the main means of getting from A to B – assuming the distance between those two points wasn't too far. It was a slow and not terribly mobile world for the average Briton.

The arrival of railways offered greater speeds than ever before. As the fledgling rail network started spreading across the nation from the 1830s onwards, it offered a more rapid means of travel for the masses. London and Edinburgh became linked by a direct line in 1850, but even the fastest trains – such as the *Special Scotch Express* of 1862 (later to become the famous *Flying Scotsman*) – took 10.5 hours for the trip, an average speed of under 40mph.

Not that there hadn't been efforts to improve the lot of those travelling on the King's highway. Britain's first self-propelled road vehicle was invented in 1801 by Cornish steam pioneer Richard Trevithick. This high-pressure steam locomotive, which didn't need rails, was christened *Puffing Devil,* but three days after carrying six passengers at a maximum velocity of 12mph, it blew up. There were subsequent attempts to build steam carriages, but the rapid spread of far more efficient and faster railways meant development was limited. Restrictive laws further hobbled British inventors. The Locomotive Act of 1861 restricted speeds to 5mph in urban areas and 10mph in the country. In 1865, the rules were made even stricter, with speed limits of 2mph in towns and cities and 4mph in rural locations, with the further requirement of a man having to walk ahead of each vehicle carrying a red flag or lantern. Such short-sighted legislation would throttle UK ingenuity for decades.

It was, therefore, left to Germany to develop what is regarded as the world's first car, with a four-stroke internal combustion engine. Karl Benz's 1885 Patent Motorwagen introduced petrol-powered personal transport to the world, and soon other nations were producing similar machines. As rudimentary as they may have been, one thing that all their creators were keen on was for them to go faster than their contemporaries; with Benz's automobile capable of just 8mph, there was great potential for that.

But with 4mph being the maximum that Brits could legally go in their own country, British engineers were slow to start developing their own versions of the horseless carriage. There was simply little incentive for them to do so. Nevertheless, what is widely regarded as the first British car appeared in 1888, in the form of the two-cylinder, two-stroke Velocycle, a tricycle with just its single rear wheel powered. But its creator, Edward Butler, wrote of it that 'the authorities do not countenance its use on the roads, and I have abandoned in consequence any further development of it'. The Velocycle was scrapped in 1896.

Therefore, it didn't really matter how capable early British cars were if attempts to take them beyond 4mph were both illegal and life-threatening to the poor chap who had to run in front with a red flag. Magazines such as *Autocar* and organisations such as the Self-Propelled Traffic Association and the Motor Car Club joined forces to battle the government, and in November 1896, a new Locomotives on

the Highways Act was passed, which removed the restrictive speed limit for any 'locomotive' under three tons. It was great news for motorists and the tiny UK auto industry alike, but only to a certain extent – the new speed limit imposed was 12mph. The Emancipation Run between London and Brighton was organised by the Motor Car Club in November 1896. It wasn't officially a race… but of course, it turned out to be. Thirty-three motorists set off from London and 17 made it to Brighton. It was, by all accounts, a chaotic and incident-packed affair, but for the 'flying escort' crowd of 10,000 or so who followed on bicycles, it ignited public interest in motorcars and what they were capable of. That the vehicle that came in first, a French Léon Bollée tricycle, managed to do so at an average speed of almost 14mph suggested that the 12mph speed limit really wasn't something that was going to be taken too seriously. The event is still commemorated today, in the form of the annual London to Brighton Veteran Car Run.

There was another shot in the arm for the British motor industry in 1900, with the staging of the Thousand Mile Trial, organised by the Automobile Club of Great Britain and Ireland, which would go on to become the Royal Automobile Club (RAC). This 15-day event saw 70 vehicles travel through major British cities between London and Edinburgh during April and May, with speed tests and hill climbs en route. Ostensibly, the regulations limited all the vehicles to an average speed of 12mph, but the gold medal went to a certain Charles Stewart Rolls – later to co-found Rolls-Royce – driving a 12hp Panhard, which managed to hit a blistering 42mph. The publicity value was huge for what could probably be regarded as the UK's first motorsport rally.

Cars were getting faster, and this was reflected in a new change in the law in 1903, when the Motor Car Act raised the speed limit to 20mph – still not fast enough for the likes of C. S. Rolls of course. There were still very few models that might be regarded as sports cars, at least in Britain. Because cars were still the preserve of the very well-heeled, companies tended to concentrate more on luxury and prestige than outright performance. Some familiar marque names had begun to appear, though. The Daimler Motor Syndicate had been founded in 1893 to build boats using Gottlieb Daimler-designed petrol engines from Germany, but when the shackles started to lift from car development, it set up a factory in the manufacturing heartland of the Midlands at Coventry to build Britain's first production model. Humber, a bicycle manufacturer, also moved from two pedal-powered wheels to four petrol-powered ones. New automobile makers proliferated; some of them established firms that had decided to branch out, others hastily formed by entrepreneurs keen to exploit the new technology for the betterment of mankind, or, more accurately, for as much money as they could get away with. The Midlands, Coventry and Birmingham, especially, provided a rich pool of manpower for these concerns. It was in this region that the fledgling car industry became consolidated and would remain so well into the future. One of those who chose Birmingham was Herbert Austin, who founded his Austin Motor Company at Longbridge near the city in 1905, having cut his teeth working for Wolseley.

At last, a distinct class of more sporting cars was beginning to emerge, spurred on by events such as the Gordon Bennett Cup. This was established by James Gordon Bennett Jr, an American newspaper tycoon, with the first race being held in France in 1900. Countries or national car clubs could send up to three cars, with the overall course covering a distance of between 340 and 400 miles. In 1902, a Napier won the Paris to Innsbruck staging. Although it had a smaller engine than its rivals, it was also lighter. This victory resulted in the establishment of one of the fundamental principles that would govern sports car design for the future; that making a car light while trying to extract as much power as possible from an engine, even if its cubic capacity was quite limited, would still result in something competitive and reliable. As a result of the win, Napier launched a racing programme and arguably became the first British manufacturer to produce vehicles that primarily focused on being sporting.

The 1903 Gordon Bennett Cup was held in Ireland. Although overall triumph went to Germany, there was another significant development in the story of the British sports car. In a nod to Ireland, the team of Brits chose Shamrock Green as the shade in which to paint their cars. This soon became established as the UK's racing colours, becoming known as British Racing Green.

In 1911, Vauxhall – a London-based Victorian engineering business that had started building cars in 1903 – launched a car with a strong claim to the title of Britain's first pure sports car, Napier notwithstanding. The Prince Henry C-type model was named in tribute to the company's success in

the 1910 Prince Henry Trials in Germany. As with the earlier Napiers, it relied less on outright power and more on effective design, but a notable feature was the streamlined bodywork, including a sharply chiselled radiator grille. Having such a halo model helped Vauxhall to sell more of its standard cars; something that many other manufacturers would come to appreciate.

In June 1907, Brooklands, the world's first purpose-built motor racing circuit, opened at Weybridge near London. The brainchild of entrepreneur Hugh F. Locke King, it was a response to the speed limit of 20mph on public roads and continuing ban on racing. There was growing concern that Britain's auto industry was being severely hampered by the lack of high-speed testing facilities. However, with Brooklands and its banked concrete 2.75-mile circuit, at last British cars could be driven to their full potential, both in races and testing. Just 11 days after the circuit opened, Napier proved their sports car credentials by taking part in the world's first 24-hour motor event, with one car setting a new world record of 1581.74 miles covered at an average speed of 65.91mph. It was the first of many records that would be set at Brooklands. Ultimately, the highest speed achieved at Brooklands would come in 1934, when a 24-litre Napier Railton managed 143.44mph.

The publicity value for marques that did well at Brooklands was also considerable. The advent of the circuit provided a vital impetus for British car makers to build more capable and performance-orientated machines, and many marques that would later become famous for their sports cars – such as Bentley and MG – would forge their reputations racing around the Surrey circuit.

However, just as the country was gaining a new confidence in car building, it all came to a sudden stop, with the outbreak of World War One in 1914. Practically every company moved over to military work and construction of private cars all but ceased – motoring for pleasure took a back seat to motoring for military purposes. However, while the conflict stunted, it also served to stimulate. Mass production methods, vital for the war effort, spread throughout the industry, and there were major advances in technology, all of which could be put to good use once the shooting had finished. By the time the war ended in 1918, the whole industry was very familiar with the benefits of properly organised and efficient assembly lines, while many more members of the public could now drive, thanks to their armed forces experiences. On top of that, after four years of hostilities and horror, there was a new appetite for fun and frivolity. The British sports cars of the Roaring Twenties, from diminutive Austin Seven Specials to thunderous Blower Bentleys, would help to fulfil those desires.

Sporting Napiers – 1901-1924

Although Napier was, for the most part, best-known for its leviathan luxury machines, it also achieved prominence in early racing by being the first British car firm to build cars especially for motorsport. Born as precision engineering company D. Napier & Sons in London in 1808, the company was facing bankruptcy by 1895. Fortunately, when Montague Napier, grandson of founder David, took over that year, the firm's focus began to shift towards the new-fangled horseless carriage. Selwyn Edge, a manager at the Dunlop Rubber Company, persuaded Napier to lightly modify his racing Panhard. Napier went further than asked, though, designing a whole new engine for it.

So impressed was Edge that he convinced Napier to start building its own vehicles. For racing during 1901, it came up with an enormous 16.3-litre-engined monster of 103bhp. It was powerful and heavy; in fact, too powerful and heavy, for when one was entered in the Gordon Bennett Cup, it soon shredded its tyres. Building on the experience, Napier dialled things back a bit for 1902, and came up with a lighter 6.44-litre car of 44.5bhp for the Gordon Bennett event. While the engine size still seems enormous by today's standards, and the power output almost laughably paltry, it was still enough for the Napier to sweep to victory (albeit with an average speed of 31.8mph over 351 miles), managing to prove more reliable than its more powerful but heavier rivals. It was the first practical demonstration that sports cars didn't just need brute force to give their best; lightness was a significant factor as well.

Bolstered by its success, Napier enthusiastically participated in racing throughout the world. However, as rivals caught up with Napier (with many of them emulating its winning formulas), its triumphs began to wane. Its last win was in the 1908 Tourist Trophy on the Isle of Man, albeit with a car badged as a Hutton instead of a Napier. Although Napier continued to build sporty models, its official racing programme ceased soon after. That said, its 12-cylinder Lion aero engine, born in 1917, found its way out of the aircraft and into several record-breaking cars such as those of Sir Malcolm Campbell and John Cobb. In the latter's Railton Mobil Special, 394mph was achieved in 1947. While Napier's own high-performance cars may have been long gone by then, the company's sporting legacy lived on by making the machines of others go very, very fast instead.

Vauxhall Prince Henry – 1911-1914

The Vauxhall Prince Henry – also known as the C-type – was in production for just three years, from 1911 to 1914. It was based on the earlier Vauxhall 20hp but with an output of 60bhp from its 3054cc four-cylinder side-valve engine and was essentially a replica of the cars that had been entered in the 1910 Prince Henry Trials in Germany. The competing Vauxhalls had greatly impressed against the foreign competition with their 65mph capability and inherent reliability during what was a tough event. Unlike many earlier cars, an attempt was made at aerodynamics, with a choice of more streamlined bodies, all of which were topped by a distinctive prow-shaped radiator grille and bonnet 'flutes' – the latter remaining a distinctive Vauxhall feature until well after World War Two. In 1913, the engine was enlarged to 3969cc, giving around 86bhp, which made 90mph possible in some models fitted with lightweight one-seater bodies. While only around 190 Prince Henry models were constructed, they established the principles for the many sports cars that would come after them and led to the Vauxhall 30-98 Velox from 1913 – regarded as the finest of all Edwardian sports cars.

Chapter 2

Roaring into the 1920s

With World War One over, Britain sought new pleasures and pastimes. The sports cars that appeared, and could finally be afforded by ordinary people, were a big part of a decadent decade.

The 1920s marked the dawn of a rosy era for the British motor industry. Horrendous as World War One was overall, Britain's young automotive industry had benefited from lucrative military contracts. Many emerged from the hostilities financially better off, and with expanded factories and upgraded production equipment. And, of course, the home bombing raids that destroyed so much infrastructure during World War Two were almost non-existent during 1914 to 1918.

In 1913, there had been 354 exhibitors at the Motor Show in London. By 1920, 512 were attending, and the following year saw 562. It was a significant expansion, fuelled by servicemen returning with military gratuities to spend, driving experience gained during the conflict and a desire to enjoy life again after the wretchedness of the past few years. However, the boom did not last long. In 1921 there was a severe economic depression that drove many manufacturers out of business. Those firms building sportier, more powerful cars received a double blow that year, with the introduction of the Road Fund Licence. More commonly known as the Horsepower Tax, this pushed manufacturers towards smaller, less complex engines, because there would be less annual duty to pay. One result of this was that many British engines were quite unreliable at sustained high speeds, and while this was less obvious in normal use on Britain's pre-motorway, slow and twisty ancient road network, it did become apparent under fast touring or racing conditions.

Therefore, during the 1920s, there was more of a focus on smaller-engined and cheaper machines, which in turn allowed more people access to motoring. The decade was dominated by the success of Austin and Morris, with the former launching what could truly be called Britain's first people's car in the form of 1922's diminutive Seven. At £225, it was within the budget of potential customers who had never owned or even seriously contemplated owning a car before. With its price reduced every year, output of the baby Austin reached 25,000 annually by 1925, its many permutations further aiding its appeal, an appeal that even extended into sports cars.

While the 747cc engine of the Seven may have been far from powerful, it was such a featherweight contraption that, even with its power output between 10bhp and 17bhp, it gave good performance. Before long, amateur and professional racers started to modify their Sevens and in 1924, even Austin itself got in on the act, introducing the Seven Sports – later to become known as the Ulster – and the Brooklands Super-Sports models in tribute to the little machine's exploits at the circuit. The Seven also formed the basis for the coachbuilt Seven Swallow of William Lyons and his Swallow Sidecar coachbuilding concern. Lyons and co. would eventually go on to form Jaguar.

There were sporty Morrises, too. Morris Garages in Oxford had an enthusiastic general manager called Cecil Kimber, who started to build his own special Morris models, with the accent on sportiness. Their badge was an octagon containing the letters 'MG' inside. By 1928, this operation had become so large and successful that it became separate from Morris Garages, becoming the MG Car Company instead. Like Jaguar, this would also become one of the most well-known and best-loved of all British sporting marques.

Other great names also started their rise to prominence during the 1920s. There was Alvis with its prestigious 12/50 tourers, while Triumph jumped from motorcycles to motorcars in 1921, starting off with the 10/20 model in 1923. Later in the decade, Riley introduced its Nine model which, with its innovative engineering, chalked up many victories in racing.

However, no chapter on the sports cars of the 1920s would be complete without a mention of two high-performance marques that are still with us today, and still represent British excellence.

Bentley Motors, named after founder Walter Owen Bentley, had its first 3-Litre prototype up and running in 1920. The cars were immediately popular with the prosperous gentlemen racers of the time, many of whom became known as Bentley Boys, in recognition of their devotion to the brand and (often) *Boys' Own* adventures with its products. It was the pre-eminent British sports car manufacturer during the 1920s, with many triumphs at Brooklands and outright wins at the Le Mans 24-Hour Races of 1924, 1927, 1928, 1929 and 1930. Bentleys became internationally renowned as a result.

Meanwhile, Aston Martin had been founded in 1913, but it only began to forge an illustrious reputation for itself during the 1920s, following an injection of cash from Count Louis Zborowski – the man who created the four Chitty Bang Bang racing cars that later inspired Ian Fleming's *Chitty Chitty Bang Bang* children's novel. That allowed Aston Martin to develop new models, which went on to compete in Grand Prix and toppled speed and endurance records at Brooklands. Ian Fleming – or at least his other famous literary creation – would go on to play a major part in the Aston Martin story several decades later. But that's a story for another chapter…

Alvis 12/50 – 1923-1932

It was the 12/50 model that established Alvis as a manufacturer of high-quality sports cars. Known for their durability and briskness, fitted with 1496cc, 1598cc and 1645cc overhead valve engines, and often carrying slimline, rakish bodywork – including 'duck's back' pointed rear ends on the Super Sports two/three-seaters, as well as later 'beetle-back' tails – the cars proved very popular with press-on private motorists as well as racers. There were several series from 1923 to 1932, with around 3,700 examples made overall.

Aston Martin 1.5-Litre – 1921-1932

The Aston Martins of the 1920s were small, almost delicate machines with engines of just 1.5 litres and power outputs of between 38bhp and 70bhp. While that might not seem much by the standards of later cars from the marque, it was enough for them to be competitive in all sorts of sporting events, with two of them contesting the Le Mans 24-Hour Race in 1928, although neither finished. However, successes elsewhere – Brooklands being a popular stamping ground – helped to ensure the cars an enthusiastic following among more financially well-off drivers. While the marketing slogan 'The premier sporting car' may have been over-egging things a little, Astons, with their refined Bertelli bodywork and towering, angular grilles, were a cut above many of their rivals.

Austin Seven Sports – 1922-1939

Austin's tiny but cheap Seven was known as the 'big car in miniature' and is widely regarded as Britain's first 'people's car'. Sports car models were offered by Austin from 1924; by 1928 there was even a supercharged two-seater that cost a mere £225. Such was the simplicity and availability of the little pocket rocket that many coachbuilders – such as Gordon England and Mulliner – also built their own racy little numbers. The concept of the small, affordable sports car began here, and would be returned to many times in the future with cars like the Austin-Healey Sprite, MG Midget and Mazda MX-5.

Bentley 4.5-Litre 'Blower' – 1927-1931

In total contrast to the Austin Seven, the 'Blower' Bentleys of the 1920s were absolute leviathans in size, performance and price. In the quest for more power, the engines of what Ettore Bugatti described as 'the world's fastest lorries' grew from 3 litres to 4.5 litres and then 6.5 litres during the decade. But it was with the fitment of a supercharger to the 4.5-Litre cars in 1929 that Bentley created a heroic British sporting legend – against the wishes of W. O. Bentley himself. While standard cars delivered 104bhp, the 'blown' versions boasted 175bhp in road form and 240bhp in racing trim, with speeds of almost 140mph possible with the latter. While 665 normally aspirated 4.5-Litre cars were made, there were just 55 Blowers. They were exclusive and exhilarating.

Daimler Double-Six – 1926-1930

Unveiled in 1926, the Daimler Double-Six was little short of monstrous. It featured Europe's first production V12 engine and was targeted at contemporary Rolls-Royces. While that put most of them in the luxury category, there were sports-bodied variants of the 3744cc and 7136cc cars. Such was their flexibility that they were noted for being able to pull from 2mph to 82mph in just top gear – albeit with a fuel consumption of around 10mpg.

Invicta 4.5-Litre – 1928-1934

Available in several forms, it was the S-Type version of the Invicta 4.5-Litre that really stood out and appealed to sports car fans. It had a low-slung chassis, which not only gave it a hunkered-down, purposeful appearance but also superb handling, thanks to its low centre of gravity. Being more a 100mph grand tourer than outright sports car, the model did better in long-distance endurance trials than it did in circuit racing, gaining a reputation for being almost indestructible.

MG M-Type Midget – 1929-1932

What the Seven was to Austin, the M-Type Midget was to Morris – but with the cachet of a somewhat more desirable badge. It was based on the 847cc Morris Minor, with a compact and appealing two-seater body. At just £175, it helped to make sports cars a more mainstream pastime. Power was quite paltry, at 20bhp to 27bhp, but that was good enough for 60mph and, in the 1920s, that was enough for most. Petite sports cars would remain a big part of the MG armoury for decades, proving that many of the best things do often come in small packages.

Riley Nine – 1926-1937

Known as the 'Wonder Car', the Riley Nine helped to establish its maker's credentials for high-quality light sporting cars. With an inventive engine featuring hemispherical combustion chambers, 45-degree-inclined valves and two camshafts, its 1087cc engine gave a good account of itself, delivering 60mph and 40mpg. The cars had featherweight but pretty fabric bodies, in open and saloon forms. Steel panelling was an option, but its extra mass dented performance. The most desirable choice was the rakish Brooklands, with pointed tail, shortened chassis and uprated engine.

Vauxhall 30/98 – 1913-1927

The Vauxhall 30/98 was a development of the previous Prince Henry and in its best-selling configuration was given the Velox suffix. While less dramatic looking than its predecessor (30/98s had gently rounded radiator grilles instead of V-shaped ones), the improved 98bhp engine allowed 100mph to be easily achievable by the lighter, racing models. Although introduced in 1913, most 30/98s were constructed during the 1920s. While the Velox had standard four-seater open bodywork, the Wensum was the most stylish, with its 'ultra-sporting body' emulating the look of a motorboat.

Rover Light Six – 1927-1932

The Rover name may not conjure up too many images of sports cars, but with its 1929 Light Six model, it did briefly shine in the performance world. The Light Six, in Sportsman saloon form, was a very attractive machine and could hit 60mph or more with its 45bhp two-litre engine. However, that didn't distinguish it too much from its rivals. What did make it stand out was when it raced France's prestigious Blue Train over 750 miles between Calais and Cannes in January 1930. It beat the train by 20 minutes, becoming the first car to do so. Enormous publicity followed.

Chapter 3
Thriving in the 1930s

Despite the decade starting with a worldwide economic depression, the 1930s proved a boom time for British sports cars – until storm clouds gathered at the end of the decade.

In 1930, the numbers of cars on British roads exceeded one million for the first time. With a national population of nearly 46 million, that might not seem many – today's figure is 38.6 million vehicles shared between over 68 million people – but it was nevertheless a significant landmark. Car ownership was spreading rapidly, with a growing trend of just motoring for pleasure – which included, for many, having something a little sportier than just a common-or-garden family runaround.

The car industry even managed to weather the economic depression triggered by the 1929 Wall Street Crash. As many other industrial concerns struggled, those building cars generally still found plenty of customers. There were exceptions, though. Some of those who specialised in expensive sports cars – such as AC, Bentley, Invicta, Lagonda, Sunbeam and Talbot – found themselves in financial straits. A few would disappear, others would be taken over by rivals. The most high-profile victim was Bentley, which was snapped up during 1931 by Rolls-Royce. The new parent company gradually diluted their sporting flavour.

Burgeoning car ownership gave rise to growing official restrictions – many of them needed. From 1931, it became compulsory to have at least third-party car insurance, while the same year saw the first *Highway Code* published, to bring some sort of order to the nation's ever-crowded roads. In 1935, driving tests were introduced. Yet output continued to increase – by the mid-1930s, Britain had overtaken France as Europe's leading motor manufacturer, producing around 403,000 machines.

MG became the nation's favourite sports car manufacturer, with an almost bewildering range of small, inexpensive buzzboxes marketed during the decade. These culminated in the first T-type, the TA, in 1936. The lineage of this model would continue through to the mid-1950s and play a significant role in making British sports cars so desirable abroad.

At the other end of the spectrum from MG was SS Cars, which had grown out of William Lyons' Swallow Sidecar concern. It started building its own fine-looking sports cars from 1932, but it was with the stunning SS100 of 1936 that enthusiasts started paying real attention to the new upstart. The name 'Jaguar' was also applied to the SS100 – a moniker that would gain even more significance for the company following World War Two.

That war, of course, would bring a sudden, decisive halt to the optimism. It would take many years for the industry, and the whole country, to recover from the calamitous events that unfolded from September 1939 onwards.

Alvis Speed 20 – 1931-1936

An archetypal 1930s British sporting grand tourer, available with factory and coachbuilt bodies, all of which were invariably graceful and imposing. With four-speed all-synchromesh 'silent' gearboxes plus independent front suspension and steering derived from Alvis' racing cars, Speed 20s had excellent road manners.

Aston Martin Le Mans – 1932-1934

After Aston Martin put in good performances in the 1931 and 1932 Le Mans 24-Hour Races, it celebrated with a Le Mans production model. Based on Aston's International cars and carrying over that range's 1494cc engine, albeit with a very creditable 70bhp, *Autocar* magazine called the Le Mans 'the closest thing to a racing car available for road use'. Praise indeed.

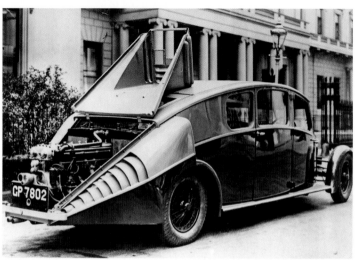

Burney Streamline – 1930-1933

This one was definitely out of left-field; a seven-seater, rear-engined aerodynamic 'wingless aircraft' that was difficult to categorise because there was just nothing else like it at the time. But with independent suspension, hydraulic brakes and 80mph from the Beverley, Lycoming and Armstrong Siddeley engines, there were definitely sporting pretensions. It was way ahead of its time.

Frazer Nash TT Replica – 1932-1938

Amid the extensive range of Frazer Nashes offered during the 1930s, the TT Replica stood out. Its name was a reference to the cars that raced in the 1931 Tourist Trophy, with the model having three engines of 1496cc, 1499cc and 1660cc over its eight-year life. One of the more idiosyncratic features was its efficient chain-drive transmission, which made it surprisingly swift and earned it the 'Chain Gang' nickname. The TT Replica especially excelled in the Alpine Trials of 1932, 1933 and 1934.

Lagonda V12 – 1937-1939

Despite winning the Le Mans 24-Hour Race in 1935, Lagonda found itself in receivership the same year. Fortunately, it was saved, and the new owner lured the great W. O. Bentley to the reborn company. The massive V12 model that came along a couple of years later was very Bentley-esque, with its new 4480cc, 180bhp V12 engine designed by W. O. and his team. It was the most powerful British engine around, but because what surrounded it was so vast, the large Lagonda was still only capable of just over 100mph. The cars were fabulous to look at, but also fabulously expensive. That they cost more than actual Bentleys must have provoked a wry smile from old W. O.

MG J3/J4 – 1932-33

MG was the master of the small sports car during the 1930s, and its J3 and J4 models were particularly special. While they shared similar looks to their siblings, their 746cc engines were supercharged. The J3 was the more civilised, intended for fast road use, but the J4 was a pure racer – coming without doors and with its engine delivering around 72bhp. At places like Brooklands, it could achieve in excess of 100mph, but even the J3 could manage about 80mph. This must have been terrifying in something so diminutive.

MG TA – 1936-1939

The MG TA was longer, wider and heavier than the Midget types that came before it, but also simpler – thanks to the switch to a tuned Wolseley 1292cc engine of 50bhp. This resulted in a car that was both faster and more reliable than its predecessors, while still perpetuating the scaled-down style that had made small MGs such hits. While purists weren't keen on it, everybody else just seemed to adore it.

Morgan F-Series – 1933-1952

Morgan had been building three-wheelers since 1911, using V-twin motorcycle engines. While they were cheap runarounds, undercutting even cars like the Austin Seven in price, they also proved pretty slick in racing. However, as four-wheeled budget rivals became cheaper and more refined, Morgan was forced to upgrade, switching to four-cylinder Ford sidevalve engines with the F-4 of 1933. There was more power, speed and sophistication. The two-seater F2 of 1935 and F Super of 1937 were the more sporting options.

Riley 12/4 Kestrel – 1935-1938

Riley gave distinctive names to its 1920s and 1930s bodies, with the Kestrel designation denoting a sporty fastback style. In 12/4 and 1.5-Litre forms from 1935, the cars were upgrades of the Nine model, with reworked twin-camshaft engines. But it was their modish, Art Deco-ish looks that really turned heads. They were very of their era.

Singer Nine Sports – 1932-1937

The Singer Nine was one of MG's great Midget rivals, with looks and performance very similar to its octagon-badged competitor. Despite only having a 972cc engine, one even managed to finish 13th overall at the 1933 Le Mans 24-Hour Race. These were very tough little things that did well in endurance events.

SS100 – 1936-1939

Probably the most renowned of all 1930s British sports cars, the SS100 was an absolute masterstroke, especially from so fresh a company as SS. The long, low and louvred SS100 – also called the Jaguar – was rakishly attractive, with a somewhat caddish air that was reinforced by the 102bhp, 2663cc and 125bhp, 3485cc engines capable of 94mph and 104mph, respectively. However, it was also very reasonably priced; at £445 for the 3.5-litre version, it substantially undercut most of its competitors. Only 198 2.5-litre examples were built, along with 116 3.5-litre ones; the low numbers reflecting both how heavily the cars were taxed and the outbreak of war rather than their huge desirability. Still, had there been more, the SS100 might not have become such a legend.

Talbot 110 – 1934-1937

The 110 was one of the last of the 'real' Talbots, being launched the year before the Rootes Group took over and, shall we say, watered things down. There was both power and refinement, with a 3377cc, 120bhp engine capable of almost kissing 100mph, and streamlined Sports tourer and Airline saloon styles that were completely up to the minute. Rootes killed the 110 off after just three years, much to the dismay of enthusiasts.

Triumph Gloria – 1934-1937

Former bicycle manufacturer Triumph started out with small cars, but the Gloria marked a move upmarket, with the company boasting it was both the 'smartest car in the land' and 'the queen of cars'. The cars clearly took contemporary Rileys for their inspiration (and main competition) and were the work of technical director and former racer driver Donald Healey. At the top of the tree was the 1991cc six-cylinder Gloria, with some very exotic-looking bodies.

Triumph Dolomite – 1937-1939

Triumph first used the Dolomite name for a spectacularly overblown and unsuccessful, supercharged eight-cylinder open sports car. It was based both mechanically and stylistically on the Alfa Romeo 8C. The title was then transferred to something a little more real world, in the form of a new line of open and closed sports cars from 1937. But Triumph was financially ailing and, in order to grab some attention, Dolomites were fitted with glitzy plunging 'waterfall' front grilles. It was probably a little much for the company's traditional customer base, and Triumph went bankrupt in 1939. Today, of course, these pre-war Dolomites are much admired for their period appearance.

Chapter 4

Fighting Through the 1940s

With war dominating half of the 1940s, sports car production was severely curtailed during the decade. But after the dust settled, British manufacturers returned with some startling designs.

All the optimism and prosperity of the 1930s rapidly evaporated with the opening years of the 1940s. As World War Two escalated, Britain stood virtually on its own and defeat seemed a very real possibility. Virtually all manufacturers were involved in government work, while civilian production dropped away. In 1939, 305,000 cars had been built in the UK; in 1940 the figure was a mere 1,949.

Aston Martin found itself making aircraft components, although it did find time to turn out one very innovative sports car, the Atom. Frazer-Nash, which had imported BMWs before the war and rebadged them, switched to gun turrets for RAF bombers instead. Lagonda became one of the largest British gun and munitions manufacturers, with a particular side-line in flame-throwers for armoured vehicles. Over at MG, amphibious tanks, trucks and aircraft were the order of the day, while Bentley – owned by Rolls-Royce since 1934 – kept itself busy with aero engines, including that most famous of wartime engineering masterpieces, the Merlin V12, as fitted to Hurricanes, Spitfires and Lancasters.

1939 to 1945 was far more damaging to British industry than World War One had been. The development of air power resulted in widescale bombing and the Midlands, as the powerhouse of Britain, found itself a major Luftwaffe target. Few companies managed to reach the end of the war with all their factories in one piece, and those with their manufacturing bases centred on Coventry were especially hard-hit. The historic city, where over 100 different companies have produced motor vehicles at one time or another, was extensively damaged during the notorious Coventry Blitz over the night of 14 November, 1940. Some companies, such as Triumph, lost everything.

After six years of conflict, Britain and its allies prevailed but the country was virtually bankrupt, with the motor industry seen as a vital way of bringing in much-needed cash. A policy, widely dubbed 'Export or Die', was introduced to sell as many cars as possible overseas. It helped lead to the explosion of interest in British sports cars in countries like the USA. American servicemen who had been stationed in the UK during the war, and enjoyed MGs and other small sports machines, either took examples home with them or bought them new once back across the Atlantic. Such popularity would persist for the next 30 years or so.

However, for the first few years after the end of hostilities, most car companies continued to build what they had been producing in the 1930s. It was only towards the end of the decade that new models emerged. Undoubtedly, the most exciting was the Jaguar XK120 of 1948. William Lyon's SS Cars had changed its name to Jaguar in 1945, keen to avoid connotations with the hated Nazi paramilitary organisation of the same name. Capable of 120mph – which made it the fastest production car in the world – it was a sleek, stylish and sensational creation, which helped set the template for all Jaguar sports cars that came after it. In austere, Blitz-ravaged, bankrupt Britain, it pointed the way towards better times just around the corner.

Allard K1 – 1946-1948

Racing driver Sydney Allard built specials before World War Two. After it, he became a motor manufacturer in his own right. His first car was the K1 of 1946. It was low-slung and aerodynamic, with a distinctive waterfall grille. Available with a 3.6-litre Ford or 3.9-litre Mercury 'flathead' V8 engine, performance was impressive for the time, putting Allard briefly in the top flight of British sports car builders.

Aston Martin Atom – 1940

Just a single Aston Martin Atom was built during 1939 and 1940. Why is it so significant, then? Well, as Europe's first concept car, it was a very progressive sports saloon, with a futuristic-looking, air-smoothed aluminium body, tubular skeleton frame chassis and independent front suspension. That it was magicked up during the darkest days of the war was quite extraordinary, especially given Aston Martin's limited resources. In 1947, industrialist David Brown bought the company, reputedly impressed after having sampled the Atom, and its basic chassis design went on to be used for the DB2, DB2/4 and DB2/4 MkIII until 1959. Without the Atom, Aston Martin may well have disappeared.

Above: Healey Silverstone – 1949-1950

Donald Healey would go on to mastermind Austin-Healey sports cars, after being Triumph's technical director during the 1930s. Immediately after the war, he set up his own business, constructing a limited series of sporting saloons, drophead coupes and two-seaters. The pick of the bunch was the Silverstone, with a light-alloy, aerodynamic body that included the headlamps behind the front grille and the rear-mounted spare wheel effectively serving as a back bumper. Power came from a 2.5-litre Riley engine. The Silverstone was a sparse, functional machine totally focussed on going fast. Just 105 were made.

Opposite above: Jaguar XK120 – 1948-1954

A worthy candidate for the title of THE stand-out British car of the 1940s – the Morris Minor notwithstanding – the Jaguar XK120 was phenomenal. Originally intended as a limited production aluminium-bodied car to test Jaguar's new six-cylinder XK engine, such was the public and press applause for what was effectively a show car that Jaguar decided to build it as a mainstream model. Its top speed was over 120mph – as the name suggested – while 60mph could be achieved in around 10 seconds. That was startlingly good performance for the era. Modified examples, for racing and rallying, were even quicker, 132.6mph being the top speed attained by one with tweaked bodywork in 1949. Initially available as a two-seater roadster from 1948, a fixed-head coupe came along in 1951, with a drophead coupe in 1953. Whatever the body style, the XK120 was embraced by the rich and glamorous on both sides of the Atlantic, as one of the most desirable cars available anywhere in the world. It was superseded by the XK140 in 1954.

Opposite below: Riley RM range – 1946-1955

Riley was taken over by the Nuffield Organisation – formed by Sir William Morris of Morris Motors – in 1938, and before long badge engineering began to dilute the marque's products. The RM range of 1946 is widely recognised as the last of the 'real' Rileys. These elegant and handsome machines, with their flowing lines, may not have been the fastest cars around – with the 1.5-litre RMA capable of 75mph and the lengthened 2.5-litre RMB able to achieve 95mph – but they looked the part and were also reasonably priced. The RMC and RMD were the 2.5-litre cars in three-seater roadster and four-seater drophead coupe form. The series had its last hurrah with the RME, an improved RMA, from 1952 to 1955, after which Rileys largely became Wolseley derivatives with a little more power.

Chapter 5

Looking Up in the 1950s

The 1950s saw the British car industry regain its strength and vitality, after the war-torn 1940s. With a degree of prosperity came a lot of new and exciting sports cars.

Although Britain entered the 1950s still facing austerity, the trials and tribulations caused by the war were gradually fading. As the country got back on its feet, the auto industry looked forward to more prosperous times – especially for those turning out sports cars.

The first few positive changes came during the final years of the 1940s, although it was only in the 1950s that their effects would start to be felt. The Brooklands circuit – where car firms had tested their cars in the 1930s – hadn't re-opened after the war. That meant there was no UK proving ground for trying out development vehicles. However, in 1946, the Motor Industry Research Association had been formed. It looked around for a site that could be shared by all manufacturers and settled on a former airfield at Lindley, near Nuneaton in Warwickshire, close to the industry's West Midlands nucleus. Specialist facilities were gradually added, enabling high-speed and endurance testing to be carried out. The MIRA site opened in 1948.

That same year, the old 1920s Horsepower Tax system was abolished. In its place was a new flat rate of £10 per car. Firms no longer felt constrained to produce small or mechanically inefficient engines in order to minimise annual duty. Whether you had the most basic Austin or expensive Aston Martin, the road fund rate was the same. It provided extra impetus for buyers to go for more powerful cars and for manufacturers to build more of them.

However, none of this meant too much while petrol was still being rationed. At a time when the Jaguar XK120 was being sold with 120mph performance, the basic petrol ration allowed the private motorist just 90 miles a month. In May 1950, rationing finally came to an end. The conditions were ideal for sports car makers; they were already selling well abroad, now there was a ready market at home as well.

Leading the field of sporting manufacturers was Jaguar. It won the Le Mans 24-Hour Race in 1951, 1953, 1955, 1956 and 1957. The publicity was invaluable at a time when success in motorsport guaranteed extra sales. Jaguar during the 1950s was selling as many cars as it could build, especially its XK range, which progressed from XK120 to XK140 in 1955, and through to the more civilised XK150 in 1958. The marque also introduced its MkI sports saloon in 1956.

An automotive giant came into being in 1952 when Austin and Morris merged to create the British Motor Corporation. BMC brought Austin, Morris, MG, Riley and Wolseley under single ownership, able to combine resources. The USA was still hungry for British sports cars, and throughout the 1950s, 80 per cent of all MG two-seaters found themselves heading over the Atlantic – a figure that would remain approximately the same, or even higher, until 1980. There was also a new BMC sports car in the form of the sensational Austin-Healey 100. The car had started life as the Healey 100, designed by Donald Healey. It used a 2.6-litre Austin engine, and when that company's boss, Leonard Lord, saw it at the 1952 Motor Show, he did a deal to build it. Production began in 1953, and the Healey acquired its Austin prefix. Later in the decade, Austin-Healey reinvented the idea of the tiny, mass-produced sports car with its 'Frogeye' Sprite.

Also in 1953, Triumph launched its curvaceous TR2, the first of the family of much-loved TR models. Sports cars were proliferating at a rapid pace. Colin Chapman produced his first Lotus, the VI, which would lead to the evergreen Seven in 1957, while Aston Martin's DB range progressed to the svelte DB4. Even Jowett, a tiny Yorkshire manufacturer, came up with one of the most distinctive sports machines of the era, the idiosyncratic Jupiter, and the first TVR burst on the scene. Along with offerings from firms such as Alvis, Bristol, Jensen, Morgan and Sunbeam, to name but a few, the 1950s was the decade when British sports cars truly came into their own.

AC Ace – 1954-1963

The smart, two-seater AC Ace certainly looked the business, with its Ferrari Barchetta-esque styling. However, early cars featured AC's antiquated six-cylinder, two-litre 100bhp engine, which didn't exactly give sparkling performance. The fitment of a Bristol two-litre 120bhp motor improved things considerably in 1956, and there was a tuned Ford Zephyr 2.6-litre unit – some with power up to 170bhp – for 1961.

Allard Palm Beach – 1952-1955

The Palm Beach was an attempt by Allard to build a less-specialised, smaller and thus cheaper machine than it had been known for in the past. The engines came from four-cylinder Ford Consuls and six-cylinder Ford Zephyrs, with the 1956 MkII offering a Jaguar 3.4-litre option. Only 80 were sold.

Alvis TD21 – 1958-1963

The post-war years saw Alvis turning out some very conservatively styled, stately saloons. However, when Swiss coachbuilder Graber came up with a new body that was far more modern, Alvis decided to adopt it. The TC108G was the first of these more up-to-date machines, with the TD21 of 1958 having slightly revised lines courtesy of Park Ward. It was one of the most dapper of 1950s grand touring Brits.

Aston Martin DB4 – 1958-1963

With a lightweight aluminium body by Carrozzeria Touring of Milan, the DB4 was a British brute in a sharp Italian suit. Its tube-frame 'superleggera' method of construction made it both strong and light, so extremely good performance could be extracted from its 3.7-litre, double-overhead camshaft engine; 240bhp gave around 140mph. However, for some that wasn't enough, and in 1959 came the DB4 GT, a lighter, higher performance variant with enclosed headlamps and 302bhp – enough to give just over 151mph, thus earning it the title of the world's fastest production road car.

Austin-Healey 100/4 – 1953-1956

The A90 Atlantic was Austin's frustrated attempt at a sports car from 1949 to 1952. It didn't do well. However, its 2660cc engine lived to fight another day, being used in the gorgeously curved Healey 100. Austin boss Leonard Lord immediately recognised a good thing when he saw it and arranged for the British Motor Corporation (BMC) to build the car under the Austin-Healey name. It was immediately popular, especially in the United States and in racing circles.

Austin-Healey 100/6 – 1956-1959

With the Austin-Healey's four-cylinder engine due to go out of production, BMC shoehorned in the six-cylinder engine from its Westminster saloon instead. Initially, this actually worsened its performance – the additional two cylinders added more weight and there wasn't that much more power. However, a new cylinder head and manifold redressed the balance somewhat. A fresh oval grille further distinguished 100/6 from its predecessor.

Austin-Healey 'Frogeye' Sprite – 1958-1961

The 'Frogeye' Sprite got its cheeky, cheerful looks accidentally – those bulging headlamps were intended to be retractable. But that would have added extra to the price of a vehicle where the whole raison d'etre was to be as cheap and accessible as possible. This was an Austin Seven Sports for the late 1950s and it kickstarted a fresh trend for inexpensive sports cars. Who cared that it was basically just an Austin A35 and Morris Minor underneath? It was just as much fun as it looked.

Bentley R-type Continental – 1952-1955

An extraordinarily beautiful and graceful automotive sculpture, the Bentley R-type Continental was more art on wheels than just a car. While the underpinnings were largely Rolls-Royce Silver Dawn, uprated engines could propel these colossi of the road to almost 120mph. But it was that gorgeous, cascading, H. J. Mulliner-styled light-alloy shape that made this Bentley so heart-stoppingly desirable.

Berkeley B60 – 1956-1957

Berkeley built caravans before it discovered sports cars, with its B60 becoming the first of a range of minuscule and minimalist glassfibre two-seaters. Two-stroke, two-cylinder motorcycle engines provided enough power to make Berkeleys seem fast without them actually being so – although by 1959, the 15bhp and 65mph of the B60 had risen to 50bhp and a frankly terrifying 105mph for something so tiny. Sadly, no more Berkeleys were sold after 1961.

Bristol 404 – 1954-1955

Bristols were always very exclusive cars, with the 404 costing twice the price of a Jaguar XK120 when launched. However, this 'Businessman's Express' did break Bristol's mould of using pre-war BMW-influenced styling, with a be-finned coupe body and distinctive 'hole in the wall' recessed grille. That there was a wood frame underneath the aluminium panels was very traditional, but that suited Bristol's customers just fine.

Gilbern GT – 1959-1967

Of the 277 Gilbern GTs produced, many were sold as kit cars to avoid purchase tax. However, the glassfibre cars from Llanwit Fardre near Pontypridd in Wales always seemed a little more grown-up than most DIY parts packages and Gilbern soon progressed to building whole cars. Underneath, there were a lot of BMC bits, including 948cc A-Series engines – which could be supercharged – or MGA B-Series units. Whatever the power source, the GT was an enthusiastic performer.

Jaguar XK140 – 1954-1957

The XK120 had been put together in a rush, never intended to be a full production model. It thus had quite a few flaws, which its successor, 1954's XK140, ironed out. The result was slightly bigger, heavier and more civilised, but lost some of the raw sporting appeal, even though there was more power on tap. The looks, in coupe, drophead and roadster form, remained largely the same – why spoil something that still looked so beautiful even after six years?

Jaguar XK150 - 1957-1961

The XK concept grew up even more with the XK150, which was even wider and heavier than before, and lost the previous undulating waistline. There was also more luxury inside. It was all still very handsome but far more a grand tourer than an outright sports car – something that would also happen to its successor, the Jaguar E-type. All-round disc brakes were a step in the right direction but, with the E-type now in development, the 150 was the XK's sunset.

Jaguar MkI – 1955-1959

Jaguar's decision to expand its range led to new 2.4 and 3.4 compact sports saloons (the MkI moniker would only be added retrospectively). The type also heralded Jaguar's entry into unitary construction. While the 2.4 cars were somewhat pedestrian, the 3.4 cars, with 210bhp, were far more potent. The rounded lines also set the styling template for Jaguar saloons well into the following decade.

541 'R' series saloon

Jensen 541 – 1954-1962

Austin running gear was used for a lot of cars from specialist manufacturers during the 1950s and the Jensen 541 was one such example. Clothing the 130bhp four-litre, six-cylinder engine and transmission from Austin's big flagship limos with aerodynamic glassfibre bodywork resulted in a very good-looking and fast car that was also unusual – the swivelling flap over the front grille being just one novel idea. So sound was the concept of a big, powerful engine enveloped by a light GRP shell that Jensen would expand on the theme for subsequent models.

Jowett Jupiter – 1950-1954

The only sports car produced by Jowett, and what a corker – a distinctive mixture of steel and aluminium panelling over a tubular spaceframe chassis, which meant that it hugged the road. The best bit was the lightweight flat-four engine of 60bhp, which sounded just delicious. The model did well at Le Mans and the Monte Carlo Rally, but Jowett's business troubles meant the Jupiter was far too short-lived.

Lotus VI – 1953-1956

Colin Chapman had been building motorsport specials since 1948 and eventually started selling kits under the name of Lotus. His VI model was intended as a racer that could also be legally driven on roads. With its spaceframe chassis clothed in alloy panels, it was extremely basic but, even with the sidevalve Ford engines that most had, performance was exhilarating thanks to minimal weight. You would never have managed 93mph in one of the cars that Ford originally fitted the 1172cc motors to.

Lotus Seven – 1957-1964

The Seven was a refinement of the VI and, with it, everything just seemed to come together. The suspension and brakes were improved, and while the Ford side-valve engines were initially carried over, there were soon the options of Ford Anglia overhead-valve and BMC A-Series units. For those who just wanted to go racing (cheaply) the Seven was ideal. The car spawned a host of imitators, with Lotus eventually selling the official rights to Caterham, which still builds it today.

MG TF – 1953-1955

By the 1950s, MG's small pre-war roadsters were well past their sell-by date. But, ahead of the MGA, there was one final update of the veteran T-type, to make the end-of-the-line MG TF look a bit more current. Compared to the preceding TD, the radiator grille was raked back, the bonnet line lowered and the headlamps blended into the wings. The bigger engine of the final TF 1500 gave a little extra oomph, but when the MGA finally laid the MG TF to rest in 1955, it was a long overdue breath of fresh air.

MG Magnette ZA/ZB – 1954-1958

The formation of BMC gave MG access to new resources, and with that came the Magnette, an elegant sports saloon based on the Wolseley 4/44 with an Austin B-Series engine in 1.5-litre form. With independent front suspension and rack-and-pinion steering, it had competent handling, even if it did take around 23 seconds to reach 60mph and maxed out at about 80mph. The ZB upgrade of 1956 increased power, meaning a top speed of 86mph and 0–60mph in 18.5 seconds.

MGA – 1955-1962

The MGA was a major leap forward for MG, a world away from the pre-war types that preceded it. It revitalised interest in the marque and was an instant success, with over 101,000 made. Initially fitted with a 1.5-litre engine, a 1.6-litre unit followed in 1959. The most exciting version was the Twin-Cam of 1958 to 1960. With a reworked double camshaft cylinder head, it was a genuinely speedy little car. Unfortunately, it also proved unreliable, which meant just 2,111 were sold.

Morgan Plus 4 – 1950-2020

The evergreen Morgan; the Plus 4 replaced Morgan's 4/4 model, looking pretty much identical, albeit with an extra four inches of wheelbase to squeeze in some rear seats. Throughout its very long life, the Plus 4 remained resolutely the same in looks, with only minor tweaks to its 1930s persona. However, engines changed from Standard to Triumph to Fiat to Rover to Ford. Although it has been a Morgan mainstay, the Plus 4 wasn't continuously in production. It was dropped in 1969, reintroduced in 1985, discontinued again in 2000 and then came back for a final run from 2005 to 2020. The name is still used today, though.

Riley One-Point-Five – 1957-1965

A car originally intended as a successor to the Morris Minor doesn't sound as if it should have much in the way of sporting credentials, but the Riley One-Point-Five was a remarkably adept little saloon. A close cousin of the Wolseley 1500, the Riley distinguished itself from it with an extra carburettor, giving 62bhp compared to the Wolseley's 43bhp. Slick handling and peppy performance meant that the Riley was more enjoyable to drive than it should have been.

Sunbeam Alpine – 1953-1955

The Alpine was the two-seater convertible sibling of the Sunbeam-Talbot 90, which distinguished itself in rallying, including winning the 1955 Monte Carlo Rally. With a soft-top instead of a tin roof, the Alpine added extra glamour. An appearance in Alfred Hitchcock's 1955 movie *To Catch a Thief*, transporting Cary Grant and Grace Kelly, cemented its reputation as a beautiful car for beautiful people.

THE *Sunbeam* ALPINE

Sunbeam Rapier – 1958-1967

Essentially the racy version of the Hillman Minx, the Rapier nevertheless raised itself above the humdrum with its flamboyant colour schemes, two-door pillarless construction and engines that had more muscle than the humbler Rootesmobiles, which shared its general appearance. It also proved it was up to the rough and tumble, with rallying successes throughout its career.

Swallow Doretti – 1954-1955

Built by the Swallow Coachbuilding Company (founded but later sold by Jaguar boss William Lyons), the Doretti was essentially a Triumph TR2 underneath but with a tubular frame chassis and aluminium panels. That made this 'special' really quite special indeed. At the time, a TR2 cost £887 while the Doretti was £1,102, so it was always going to be a niche product, but it is commonly believed that pressure from other car makers brought a premature end to the project after just 250 cars. Shame...

Triumph TR2 – 1953-1955

The TR2 was a simple, but very effective, little weapon. There wasn't much to it, with just a basic voluptuous body over a ladder-type chassis and the two-litre engine from the Standard Vanguard, boosted by an extra carburettor. However, this first TR seemed greater than the sum of its parts; tough, reliable and, above all, tremendously lively to drive. The USA especially loved it. Triumph made sure that the car had a high profile in motorsport and speed record attempts, which in turn attracted buyers.

Triumph TR3/3A – 1955-1961

In 1955, the TR2 was upgraded into the TR3. There were minor improvements such as better ventilation, more room inside, marginally more power and a different grille. The big news was that, after a year, the TR3 became the first British car to be fitted with front disc brakes as standard. The TR3A popped up in 1957 with a full-width grille and the decadence of external door handles.

Above: TVR Grantura – 1958-1966

TVR, founded by Trevor Wilkinson (TVR taking its name from 'Trevor'), had been around since 1946, but it was with the Grantura that people started to sit up and take notice. The individualistic glassfibre shell, hand-built in Blackpool, masked a very low chassis with Volkswagen Beetle-type suspension and a choice of engines of varying intensity, including Coventry Climax, Ford and MG. While the Grantura shape would evolve over the years, it could still be distinguished in the models that were being built in the late 1970s.

Right: Wolseley 6/90 – 1954-1959

The Wolseley 6/90 wasn't a true sports saloon but it was, at least, based on the Riley Pathfinder, which was marketed as one. With a six-cylinder engine – the Riley had a four-pot one – from the Austin Westminster, the Wolseley was a credible performer and its widespread police use gave it the veneer of speed and authority that doubtless attracted some who might otherwise have gone for a more performance-orientated marque.

Chapter 6

Swinging into the 1960s

British sports cars reached their peak during the 1960s. It was the decade that gave us the Jaguar E-type, the Aston Martin DB5, the MGB… and much more besides.

The 1960s are fondly remembered, perhaps through somewhat rose-tinted spectacles, as the best decade of the 20th Century. It was a colourful era noted for its wonderful music, fantastic cinema and TV, vibrant fashions, significant social and cultural progressions… and some of the best-loved British cars of all time.

The British motor industry was second only to the USA's in the 1960s. In 1963, over two million vehicles left British factories, bound for showrooms across the globe. Motoring by now was for everyone; personified by cars like the Mini and Ford Cortina. While both these cars were intended as family machines, sporty variants were also launched that went on to become legends in their own right, in the form of the Mini Cooper and Lotus Cortina. The policy of offering 'hot' versions of humble saloons became commonplace during the 1960s and would continue in the following decades.

There were also more 'proper' sports cars than ever before. One of the world's most popular sports cars was launched by MG in the form of the MGB, while the smaller Midget – a revival of a pre-war name – satisfied the budget end of the market. But MG had its rivals; most notably Triumph, which pitched its Spitfire against the Midget and its GT6 against the MGB GT. Lotus was also now a major contender, having fully shed its kit car image with the Elan, a car that established a new benchmark for handling prowess and also helped popularise that most essential of all classic sports cars features, pop-up headlamps.

Any of these cars would have made the 1960s stand out, but there were two giants of the decade that today, over half a century on, still vie for the title of the greatest British sports car ever made. Jaguar unleashed its E-type, a car that was sensational in both looks and performance. With a 150mph top speed and the most stunning design of any sports car before or since, it became an icon of its era. The same could be said of Aston Martin's DB5, although its fame came more from its appearance alongside Sean Connery as James Bond in *Goldfinger,* adding another link between Bond's creator, Ian Fleming, and Aston Martin, in addition to *Chitty Chitty Bang Bang*. As THE car most associated with 007 – and still used in the most recent movies including *No Time To Die* – it has become the most famous car in the world.

There was one particular bonus for sports cars owners during the 1960s, and that was the rapid spread of the motorway network. At first, there was no speed limit, until AC was reputedly caught testing one of its Cobra Coupes at 185mph on the M1 one morning in 1964. The 70mph speed restriction promptly followed but, nevertheless, the new motorways gave sports car enthusiasts plenty of opportunity to properly stretch their machines' legs.

AC Cobra – 1961-1967

The Cobra was an astounding Anglo-American collaboration, which saw AC and US racing driver and designer Carroll Shelby team up to squeeze a Ford V8 into the Ace. What resulted was one of the most brutal sports cars ever, especially post-1965 when a 6997cc V8 became available. Its 410bhp allowed an alarming 165mph for the very brave or very foolish.

Alvis TE21/TF21 – 1963-1967

The final Alvises kept the basic TD21 shape but added very fashionable vertical twin headlamps, giving these imposing machines even more road presence. With the final TF21, power rose from 130bhp to 150bhp. After the demise of the TF21, Alvis concentrated on building military machines under new owner Rover.

Aston Martin DB5 – 1963-1965

The DB5 was an evolution of the DB4 and, while it was a great car in its own right – with the trendy faired-in headlamps of the DB4 GT and 282bhp as standard – it was its appearance in 007 films *Goldfinger* and *Thunderball,* plus the subsequent gadget-laden Corgi model, that propelled it to superstardom. It was, though, every bit as handsome as Sean Connery and, in 314bhp Vantage form, just as deadly.

Aston Martin DB6 – 1965-1971

The final evolution of the DB4/DB5 shape saw increasing civilisation and sophistication in the form of the DB6. Thanks to an increased wheelbase and raised roofline, there was space for four passengers, while the Kamm tail improved the aerodynamics and handling. In Vantage form, 325bhp was available. The drophead coupe variant was dubbed the Volante from 1967 onwards.

Aston Martin DBS – 1967-1973

A radical change of shape for Aston Martin, the DBS moved away from Italian lines to a more American muscle car profile, courtesy of British designer William Towns. The car was intended to come with a V8 engine, but that wasn't ready in time, and so the DB6's six-cylinder unit was fitted instead. Even when the V8 was ready, the six-cylinder DBS continued until 1973 as a 'budget' Aston.

Austin-Healey 3000 MkIII – 1964-1968

The last of the 'Big' Healeys was the best, certainly if you liked a few creature comforts. It had the most power, with 148bhp, plus a more luxurious interior with a wooden dash. Later Phase 2 cars had a revised suspension set-up, better to cope with the 121mph potential. There were no more 3000s after 1968, which caused much dismay among British sports car fans.

Austin-Healey Sprite – 1961-1971

The reworked Austin-Healey Sprite lost its distinctive 'frogeye' headlamps but added an opening boot – although the 'luxuries' of wind-up windows and exterior door handles weren't lavished on customers until 1964. The 948cc engine went up to 1098cc in 1962, with 1275cc following in 1966 – by which point this tiny sports car could achieve almost 100mph. The Sprite was dropped in favour of the MG Midget in 1971, but it was exactly the same car save for the badging.

Bond Equipe – 1963-1970

A Bond car of a different type; while the Equipe was no Aston Martin, it did a pretty adept job of putting a sporty glassfibre body on a Triumph Herald chassis while allowing room for four people inside – just about. The early cars used Spitfire engines and had single headlamps up front, but from 1964 there were twin lamps, which improved the looks somewhat. In 1967, Bond built a new, more square-rigged version with the two-litre engine from the Vitesse giving 100mph capability.

Bristol 408 – 1964-1965

Bristol started to use Chrysler V8 engines from 1962 with its 407 model. The 408 improved on its immediate predecessor with a lower profile and a wider grille (which also had two lamps set into it). There were 250bhp to play with from its 5130cc American powerhouse, meaning the 408 could reach over 125mph.

Daimler SP250 'Dart' – 1959-1964

While its official designation was SP250, this intriguing and idiosyncratic open two-seater from Daimler was better-known as the Dart, the name it was originally intended to be called. With a glassfibre body and masterful British-designed 2.5-litre V8, it had very good performance, even if the looks were a bit Marmite for many. After Jaguar took over, it improved the somewhat shaky roadster but then killed it off in 1964 to protect E-type sales. Just 2,650 were constructed.

Ford Lotus Cortina MkI – 1963-1966

Ford's Cortina MkI wasn't a sports car, it was intended as family transport, something it excelled at. However, when Lotus dropped its twin-cam engine – derived from Ford's Kent motor, as used in humbler Cortinas – into what was quite a lightweight bodyshell, it did create something that would go on to become a sports car legend. With the running gear also reworked, the Lotus Cortina excelled in saloon car racing but also made an extremely practical fast road car.

Ford GT40 – 1964-1969

The GT40 was primarily a racing car, but a small number of road-going cars were put together. This Anglo-American collaboration was little short of epic, with bodywork that was only 40 inches high – hence the name – and mid-mounted V8 engines. Its whole reason for existence was so that a vengeful Ford could beat Ferrari in top-flight motorsport, which it ultimately did. The fact that a by-product was a street-legal Ford that could hit 154mph and go from zero to 100mph in under 12 seconds was just a big bonus.

Ford Capri MkI – 1969-1974

After the success of the Mustang in the USA it was only a matter of time before Ford tried something similar in Europe. The Capri was totally inspired by its American relation, with a range of engines from mediocre to mighty and a lengthy options list, so cars could be personalised until an owner's heart was content. Engine sizes ranged from four-cylinder 1298ccs through to 3091cc V6s on the MkI, which meant there was a Capri option for everybody. 'The car you always promised yourself' proved a runaway success.

Gilbern Invader – 1969-1974

Developed from the Gilbern Genie, these handsome Welsh glassfibre sports saloons used MG steering and suspension mated with a 2994cc Ford Zephyr V6. There was even an estate version later in the Invader's life, which proved a very swift way of lugging loads around.

Right: Gordon-Keeble – 1964-1967

Styled by the great Giorgetto Giugiaro, the Gordon-Keeble was one of the decade's best-looking British cars, thanks in part to that stylish slanted quad-headlamp nose – at a time when few other manufacturers were doing such things. It also combined a Chevrolet Corvette 300bhp engine with glassfibre bodywork, so both handling and performance were impeccable, with 0-60mph in 7.5 seconds and an ultimate velocity of 136mph. Only 99 were made; the car deserved better.

Below: Jaguar Mk2/240/340 – 1960-1969

Jaguar's facelift of its MkI sports saloon was a masterclass in how to do revamps properly. The Mk2 lost much of the thick-set dumpiness of the MkI with more glasswork, deeper windscreen and wider rear track. It looked more elegant and slimmer. Best of all was that Jaguar's 3781cc XK engine joined the existing 2483cc and 3442cc line-up. The Mk2 became almost as redolent of fast motoring in the 1960s as Jaguar's other great of the era, the E-type. Speaking of which...

Jaguar E-Type Series I/II – 1961-1971

The most beautiful sports car ever born? The E-type had everything going for it; alluring long-bonnet looks, a top speed of 150mph (or at least close to that), superior handling and a price that undercut most of its competitors. It became the car to be seen in during the 1960s, and even the loss of the cowled headlamps in 1967 didn't dent the E's appeal with buyers. The car is just as desirable today.

Jensen C-V8 – 1962-1966

Having turned to glassfibre with its previous 541, Jensen continued with the material for its striking C-V8. While the car was largely a 541 from the windscreen back, the transformation to a shark-like quad-headlamp nose gave the C-V8 a dramatic new face. The drama didn't stop there; enormous Chrysler V8 engines were also fitted, first a 5916cc one of 305bhp and then a 6276cc, 335bhp motor, making this Jensen a 140mph machine.

Jensen Interceptor – 1966-1976

Jensen ditched the glassfibre for its 1966 Interceptor, but kept the Chrysler V8. The bodies were designed by Touring of Milan but initially built by Vignale in Italy before Jensen brought everything back to the UK. Very imposing lines – including the huge curved glass hatchback – were complemented by remarkable performance from something so big. The SP (Six-Pack) offered more power courtesy of its three twin-barrel carburettors, while the FF featured four-wheel drive at a time when the format was more usually limited to Land Rovers and tractors.

Lotus Elan – 1962-1973

Lotus boss Colin Chapman knew how to make cars handle, and with the Elan, he proved that beyond all doubt. The pretty glassfibre body would have been enough to make the Elan stand out, especially with the talking point of pop-up headlamps, but the backbone chassis and independent suspension made this grown-up Lotus the master of any road. It could run rings around practically anything else. In addition to the roadster, there was a coupe and stretched 2+2 – dubbed the Plus 2 – as well as the Sprint with a tweaked engine.

Marcos 1800/1500/1600 – 1964-1968

With a laminated plywood chassis, glassfibre body and Volvo 1783cc engine, the Marcos was already unusual before you even got to the undulating low-profile appearance. It was aimed at the sort of driver who might otherwise have bought an MG. Thanks to Volvos still being uncommon in Britain at the time, more readily available and cheaper Ford 1498cc and 1599cc engines were later adopted. It was one of the more idiosyncratic sports cars of the 1960s, and all the better for that.

Marcos Mini-Marcos – 1965-1974

When the Mini was given the Marcos glassfibre treatment it created a potent pocket rocket of a car. The shape may not have been conventionally attractive but it had very good aerodynamics and, thanks to the use of Mini components underneath, the car's road manners were impeccable, even if the top speed was only about 75mph. A sports car for those on a budget who appreciated the quirky.

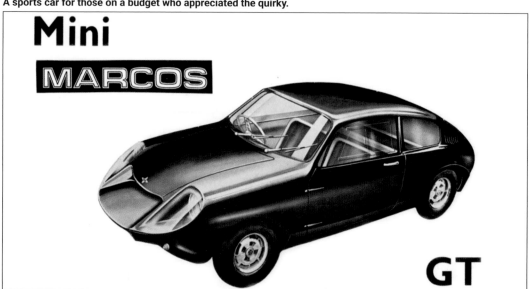

MG Midget – 1961-1979

The MG-badged variant of the Austin-Healey Sprite provided exactly the same big fun in a small package as its sibling (and rival). However, it outlived the Healey by eight years, with engines over the years including 948cc, 1098cc, 1275cc and 1493cc – the latter courtesy of another competitor, the Triumph Spitfire, during the mid-1970s. One thing that didn't change was the car's diminutive dimensions.

MGB – 1962-1980

One of the world's most popular and enduring sports cars, the MGB had mass appeal right from the start. While it wasn't quite as lovely as the preceding MGA in looks, it built on that car's good points with a bigger 1798cc B-Series engine and front disc brakes as standard. The MGB just did everything well, yet at a very reasonable price. Initially, only a roadster was available, but a tin-top coupe was introduced in 1965. With cosmetic changes for better and worse, but always the same 1.8-litre engine, the MGB would survive right until the start of the 1980s.

MGC – 1967-1969

After the demise of the Austin-Healey 3000, BMC attempted to repeat the trick with the MGC, an MGB fitted with the corporation's six-cylinder 2912cc C-Series engine. While it created a car that was in the spirit of the previous Austin-Healey, with similar 120mph performance, the heavy engine didn't do anything for handling, and buyers were also less than keen on a car that looked so much like a standard MGB.

Mini Cooper – 1961-1971

The basic Mini was such a fine-handling car that it was almost inevitable a performance version would appear – even if the man behind the Mini, Alex Issigonis, didn't want it. Fortunately, F1 car constructor John Cooper ignored him and came up with a tweaked Mini. Named the Mini Cooper in tribute, the ultimate incarnation was the 76bhp, 1275cc S, which became a Monte Carlo Rally legend. With a top speed of 96mph, Coopers weren't that fast on straights but they were unbeatable on bends.

Morgan Plus 8 – 1968-2004

Take a Morgan and shoehorn a Rover V8 engine in its front. That's what the company did in 1968, coming up with one of the most enduring classic British roadsters in the process. It still looked like all the other Morgan models – the marque having created a nice retro-styled niche for itself – but it went far better thanks to the V8's 161bhp. 120mph in something that looked so pre-war was impressive.

Sunbeam Rapier – 1967-1976

The British Plymouth Barracuda? The Rapier was the 'hot' version of the new Alpine of 1967, a derivative of the Hillman Hunter. Both these fastback Sunbeams shared a distinct resemblance to the Plymouth from over the Atlantic, as Chrysler owned both brands. The H120 variant was the most desirable, with a tuned 1725cc engine and Rostyle wheels.

Triumph Spitfire -1962-1980

Triumph's answer to the MG Midget and Austin-Healey Sprite was a neat little machine that made good use of the Herald chassis, albeit in shortened form. It also appealed to Brits because of its World War Two fighter-inspired name – rather more stirring than Midget or Sprite. Its long production life would see it survive through to 1980, going from 1147cc to 1296cc to 1493cc during its 18-year existence.

Triumph Vitesse – 1962-1973

Triumph was the master at recycling its Triumph Herald platform and, while the Vitesse looked quite a lot like the car it took as its basis, the slanted quad-headlamps marked it out as something a bit beyond the humdrum. Drivers also got extra from the 1596cc six-cylinder engine, which was enlarged to 1998cc in 1966. Road manners could be a little wayward on the early cars, but Triumph did try to improve things over the years.

Triumph GT6 – 1966-1973

Known as 'the poor man's E-type', this further example of just how versatile the Herald chassis was shared certain characteristics with the larger, more exotic sports car. Both had six-cylinder engines, a similar undulating waistline and fastback styling with an opening rear hatch. The GT6 was clearly a tin-top offshoot of the open-top Spitfire but its 1998cc engine gave it longer legs, justifying the GT designation.

Triumph TR4/TR4A – 1961-1967

For 1961, Triumph's favourite Italian stylist, Giovanni Michelotti, restyled the TR3. The TR4 was both wider and more sophisticated, and looked much more 1960s than 1950s. It also featured a few more creature comforts. To maintain performance for what was now a heavier car, the engine was enlarged from 1991cc to 2138cc. Things got better still with the TR4A of 1964, which had independent rear suspension fitted.

Triumph TR5 – 1967-1969

Things got really serious with the TR range in 1967, when the TR5 got treated to a 2498cc six-cylinder engine with Lucas fuel injection, as used in Triumph's executive saloon range. Top speed and acceleration improved considerably as a result. In most other respects, the TR5 remained the same as the previous TR4A, but definitely felt more special.

Triumph TR6 – 1969-1976

The TR6 was a clever revamp of the existing TR5. Triumph needed fresher looks and, because Michelotti was busy, the design went to German firm Karmann instead. It revised the front and rear ends while leaving the centre tub alone, and voila – Triumph had a TR that looked good enough for the coming decade. There were next to no mechanical changes.

Chapter 7

Turbulent Times in the 1970s

Nothing seemed to go that right for British sports car manufacturers in the 1970s. There were fuel crises, new rules abroad and industrial strife at home to deal with. Despite all this, speeds increased and styling got sleeker, with some cars approaching supercar status.

After the heyday of the 1960s, it is surprising, even shocking, just how quickly things went haywire during the 1970s. It was a time of employee unrest, poor management, financial woes and dubious quality control. Few look back on the cars of the era as that well-made and reliable.

Just before the start of the decade, the British Leyland Motor Corporation came into existence, grouping three of Britain's mainstream sports car manufacturers – Jaguar, MG and Triumph – under the same industrial umbrella, alongside a vast range of less-specialised family and commercial vehicles. Many of the cars were now internal rivals for each other – in the case of MG and Triumph quite bitter ones, with the Midget directly pitched against the Spitfire, and MGBs and TRs also vying for supremacy. Because British Leyland was so vast, the various divisions found themselves fighting for resources, while others were dispensed with – Riley being wound up in 1970 and Austin-Healey disappearing in 1972. Development of cars like the MGB stagnated during the 1970s and where there were changes – such as the fitment of black 'rubber' bumpers on MGBs to meet new US safety regulations – they were hardly greeted with unbridled enthusiasm.

That is not to say there weren't some significant new sports cars from the BL stable. The Jaguar XJ-S replaced the long-in-the-tooth E-type, while Triumph came up with the four-seater convertible Stag, the superb-but-flawed jewel that was the Dolomite Sprint and the modern yet controversial TR7, with its distinctive wedge profile. However, because of the turmoil at British Leyland, build quality and reliability often left a lot to be desired, which did nothing for reputations or ongoing sales.

The troubles of the time seem to spread through the industry. Aston Martin changed hands in 1972 and went into receivership in 1974 but managed to cling to life after being saved by a business consortium. Jensen also folded in 1976, after a brief tie-up with Donald Healey to create the Jensen-Healey as a possible Austin-Healey replacement. It didn't succeed, despite the car being quite a fascinating beast.

There were success stories, though. Lotus moved upmarket from its small, stark track cars with more sophisticated offerings such as the Eclat, Elite and Esprit. The latter had mid-engined supercar looks to match the best from Italian rivals such as Ferrari, Lamborghini and Maserati, even if overall performance was a little lacking. It was Ford that really shone during the decade. Buoyed up by the buyer appeal of its family Escorts and Cortinas, it produced a number of high-performance saloons and revamped the Capri into the very popular MkIII form, an object lesson in how to make what was a great car even better.

The 1970s was one where manufacturers generally had to compromise rather than innovate, with fuel crises and spiralling safety legislation to deal with. Nevertheless, the decade still saw some stunning and sometimes even startling sports cars appear in Britain.

AC 3000ME – 1979-1984

The 3000ME was a complete change of direction at AC compared to its previous machines. It had a mid-mounted Ford V6 engine and exotic looks that suggested it should be capable of more than the 120mph it could actually achieve. That it was first shown in 1973 but took until 1979 to go on sale didn't help, either. AC had high hopes but only 82 were sold.

Aston Martin V8 – 1972-1990

Aston Martin's mainstay during the 1970s and 1980s was its V8 saloon, effectively a British muscle car with a 5340cc V8 plus, naturally, fine attention to the interior details. Even in standard form, it was luxurious and very, very quick, but it was with the Vantage version of 1977 that things went truly wild; 170mph and zero to 60mph in 5.4 seconds propelled this British bruiser into supercar territory. The Volante was the convertible version – and what a way to get a lot of wind in your hair.

Aston Martin Lagonda – 1977-1990

This extraordinary and lavish leviathan was a technological tour de force with almost shocking, razor-edged, wedge-shaped styling. It looked like a spaceship in the mid-1970s and, with the same 5340cc V8 as Aston's more conventional sports cars, it went like one as well. It was way ahead of its time – in fact, too much so, for all the electronics proved unreliable and were eventually made less complex so they actually did what they were supposed to. Remarkably, given the Lagonda's very of-its-era appearance, it lasted through to 1990.

Bristol 412 – 1975-1982

The 1970s was one of the 21st Century's stranger decades, which perhaps goes to explain why Bristol eschewed all the curves of its previous cars for the remarkable 412 in 1975. The blunt, breeze-block appearance was courtesy of Italian coachbuilder Zagato. There was little in the way of aerodynamics but, with a 335bhp 6556cc V8, they weren't that needed – the 412 could still hit 140mph, projecting a shock-and-awe image while doing so.

Caterham Seven – 1974-present

The Lotus Seven was reborn, albeit now built by Caterham after it bought the rights from Lotus in 1973. The car has remained remarkably true to its roots and still looks much the same today as it always has, but assorted Ford, Rover and Vauxhall engines have been used over the years to make it go – and go a Caterham Seven certainly does. It remains one of the purest driver's cars on sale.

Clan Crusader – 1971-1974

The Mini had been adapted for all manner of sporty specials almost from its inception, but its chief British rival, the Hillman Imp, saw less such use. However, the Clan Crusader did take the Rootes Group's bijou rear-engined runaround as its basis and proved rather effective, getting 100mph out of just 51bhp. The pointy glassfibre body wasn't to everybody's taste but the Clan definitely looked different to all its rivals.

Ford Escort MkI RS1600/ Mexico/RS2000 – 1970-1974

Ford established an Advanced Vehicle Operations division in 1970 for special projects, and the RS1600 was one of its first fruits. It had a very specialised 120bhp, 16-valve, 1601cc Cosworth BDA twin-cam engine developed from a Formula Two racing engine. Even with a heavier Escort shell around it, nearly 120mph was possible. The Escort Mexico and RS2000 were based on the RS1600 but with more conventional (and thus more reliable) Kent and Pinto engines. These had less power but compensated with more flamboyant colours and graphics.

Ford Escort RS2000 MkII – 1976-1980

When the Escort transformed from MkI to MkII in 1975, Ford continued to offer sporty versions, although it did seem that the focus was now more on lairy looks that genuine ability. That said, the 110bhp MkII RS2000 still boasted semi-sparkling performance and also had considerable pose value thanks to its streamlined 'droop snoot' nose.

Ford Capri III – 1977-1986

The Capri MkII had added a hatchback to Ford's European Mustang wannabe. The MkIII, just four years later, smoothed out the body so effectively that the car looked much fresher than its 1960s origins – and quad headlamps always look great on a sports car. With the Blue Oval's fuel-injected 2792cc 'Cologne' V6 engine fitted from 1981, the Capri MkIII seemed much younger than it actually was.

Hillman Avenger Tiger – 1972-1973

The Hillman Avenger Tiger looked fast and was… well, quite fast. The bright Sundance Yellow livery with black detailing and alloy wheels certainly made it difficult to ignore, while the twin-carb 1498cc engine meant it could get to 60mph from rest in under 10 seconds and max out at 108mph. That made it quicker than Ford's Escort Mexico. The MkII version of late 1972 introduced quad round headlamps and Wardance Red as an alternative to Sundance Yellow.

Jaguar E-type Series III – 1971-1975

A bigger, more bulgy body made the Series III E-type much less the lithe sports car it had once been, but the smooth new V12 engine restored some of the vigour that had been lost since the early 1960s. Much more a grand tourer than its six-cylinder predecessors, this final incarnation kept the E alive in its main US market – at least until the 1973 fuel crisis made it patently clear just how thirsty it was. Purists may not like the Series III but it was what was needed at the time.

Jaguar XJ-S – 1975-1996

One of the problems with the XJ-S was that it officially replaced the E-type, yet didn't replace it at all. It was a completely different kind of machine to the legend it came after, and those expecting a return to an outright sports car were disappointed – the XJ-S was always intended to be a long-limbed grand tourer. Still, it matured nicely and was still being built in 1996, suggesting that Jaguar had done quite a good job despite the critics (who fixated rather too much on the buttressed rear window).

Jensen-Healey – 1972-1976

The thinking behind the Jensen-Healey was that it could neatly fill the void left by British Leyland's axing of the Austin-Healey brand. Unfortunately, it didn't manage it – the initial unreliability of the new Lotus 1973cc 16-valve twin-cam engine did not help matters. Other bits came from Vauxhall (suspension and steering) and Chrysler (gearbox). It is more appreciated now than in its day.

Jensen GT – 1975-1976

The departure of Donald and Geoffrey Healey from Jensen meant that the company's sporting estate variant of the convertible Jensen-Healey was just known as the Jensen GT. Most of the mechanics were the same, except for a Getrag five-speed gearbox, but the extended roof added novelty and practicality. There was also extra luxury in the cabin compared to the convertible.

Lotus Europa Twin-Cam/Special – 1971-1975

Although the first mid-engined Lotus Europas appeared at the tail end of the 1960s, it was only with the Twin-Cam/Special models of 1971 that the type reached anything like its proper potential. Lotus' effervescent twin-cam 1558cc engine replaced the previous underpowered Renault motors, giving 105bhp (Twin-Cam) or 126bhp (Special). Mid-engined, road-going sports cars were still a rarity at the time and the Europa was something very different to the norm.

Lotus Elite – 1974-1980

A Lotus for adults; the Elite could fit in four adults and swallow most of their luggage as well, thanks to its opening glass hatchback. This attempt at a sporty estate didn't have the happiest styling – it seemed too truncated at the rear – but it was practical and aerodynamic, especially with those pop-up headlamps.

Lotus Eclat – 1975-1980

Criticisms about the shape of the Elite led to the Eclat one year later. This had fastback coupe styling but remained the same mechanically as its more spacious older sister. The model was reborn as the Excel in 1982.

Lotus Esprit – 1976-1987

Lotus magicked up one of THE cars of the decade with the Esprit. Giorgetto Giugiaro did the fabulous wedge-shaped styling, which wouldn't have disgraced a Ferrari. There was 'only' a 1973cc twin-cam engine but, because it was mid-mounted and on a backbone chassis with a glassfibre body, the Esprit clung on in corners like little else. 135mph from 160bhp meant this Lotus fell a little short of the supercar abilities its looks suggested, but neither did normal versions turn into submarines, as one did for Roger Moore's 007 in *The Spy Who Loved Me*.

Marcos Mantis – 1970-1972

This four-seater Marcos was intended to broaden the appeal of the specialist sports car manufacturer. While it did have quite a lot going for it – such as the trusty Triumph TR6 2498cc six-cylinder engine – the unfortunate resemblance to a snuffling anteater didn't win it many friends. Only 32 were sold. Age hasn't improved the aesthetics, but they are certainly a curiosity today.

MG Midget 1500 – 1974-1980

The final MG Midgets deserve an entry all to themselves here because they were so altered from the 1960s and early-1970s ones that preceded them. The black plastic bumpers were a safety feature to meet American legislation, while the Triumph Spitfire 1493cc engine was more able to meet American emissions rules. It made the Midget a 100mph car at last, but few people felt the new front and rear protuberances enhanced the cosmetics, while the raised ride height didn't do much for the handling.

MGB – 1974-1980

The so-called 'rubber bumper' MGBs (actually, the material was polyurethane) were a necessary evil so that the model could continue to be sold in the USA. In reality, they blended quite well with the MG's overall shape and did a neat trick of updating the ageing appearance in the process. Nevertheless, enthusiasts bemoaned the loss of the chrome, the raised suspension height, and the falling power. The best days of the MGB were now long behind it, and the end was nigh.

MGB GT V8 – 1973-1976

Following on from the earlier six-cylinder MGC, British Leyland went two further with the MGB GT V8 of 1973 to 1976, dropping in its 3528cc Rover V8. It was a more well-rounded car, as the Rover V8 was lighter than the six-pot C-Series found in the MGC. So the GT V8 – there were no official convertibles, incidentally – behaved itself better, and was also faster, with 125mph achievable. However, with typical BL luck, the car was launched in the middle of a fuel crisis which robbed it of the sales it deserved.

Morris Marina 1.8TC – 1971-1975

British Leyland tried to grab some of the Ford Capri market with the Marina 1.8TC by fitting twin-carb 1798cc engines in the same state of tune as in MGBs to coupes and saloons. That made them fast in a straight line, up to 100mph. However, the Marina's notorious understeer meant that bends had to be treated with much slower respect.

Panther J72 – 1972-1981

If you were a Jaguar fan who wasn't keen on the Jaguar E-type Series III or the XJ-S that came after it, then the Panther J72 was for you. It harked back to the glory days of the SS100 in appearance but made use of Jaguar six-cylinder XK and V12 engines for propulsion, resulting in a pre-war persona with post-war performance. Many celebrities loved them but the overall impression was of something lacking in taste. Still, it was the 1970s...

Panther Lima – 1976-1982

To make Panther a little more mainstream, the company took on Morgan with the Lima, albeit with glassfibre bodywork. Vauxhall supplied most of the bits under the roadster shell, including the 2279cc engines. For a Panther it sold quite well, with 897 made before the similarly themed Kallista superseded it in 1982.

Reliant Scimitar GTE (SE6) – 1975-1986

Reliant's sporty load-lugger made its first appearance in 1968 but was revamped in 1975 with a more executive image. The SE6 was both widened and given a longer wheelbase, which upped the amount of space inside. Equipment levels and luxury were also improved. Ford V6 engines gave these plush, practical shooting brakes a nice turn of speed too.

Talbot Sunbeam-Lotus – 1979-1981

A hot hatch with a difference; unlike most late 1970s and early 1980s fast hatchbacks, the Sunbeam Lotus was rear-wheel drive instead of having its front wheels powered. That is because it was based on the a shortened Hillman Avenger floorpan, with Lotus brought in to make it suitable for rallying – which included adopting Lotus' 2174cc 16-valve 150bhp engine. Success in national and international rallying gave Talbot considerable publicity, but not enough to save owner Peugeot from axing the marque in the mid-1980s.

Triumph Stag – 1970-1977

The Stag was a car that should have been a European, or even a world, star. As a 2997cc V8-powered four-seater convertible with very handsome Italian lines by Giovanni Michelotti, it had everything going for it when unveiled in 1970. Sadly, the brand new V8 engine suffered from too many reliability issues, which put off buyers. Consequently, the Stag never lived up to its potential. Today, though, its foibles are much better appreciated and solved.

Triumph Spitfire 1500 – 1974-1980

The final genesis of the Triumph Spitfire saw it fitted with the same 1493cc engine as the last MG Midgets, thus bringing these two in-house British Leyland rivals even closer together – customers might have well just tossed a coin to choose between them. Like the Midget, the Spitfire was clearly long-in-the-tooth by the mid-Seventies, but there was still a lot of entertainment and excitement to be gained from something so small that could manage 100mph.

Triumph Dolomite Sprint – 1973-1980

Another great Triumph missed opportunity; the Dolomite Sprint was a real attempt to make the Dolomite executive saloon into something truly sporty. The Sprint's 127bhp 16-valve engine transformed the Dolly into a 115mph weapon with lively characteristics, but it was also too clever for its own good, and without proper care and attention, it proved quite fragile. This outweighed its abilities in the eyes of many potential customers. Like its Stag stablemate, there is now more understanding of its pros and cons, and the pros win out these days.

Triumph TR7 – 1975-1981

The six-cylinder TR5s and TR6s were very macho machines, but the TR7 was more polished. Instead of six cylinders, it only had four, and 1998cc instead of the 2498cc of the past. There was also no convertible option at first – it didn't arrive until 1979 – and the divisive wedge-shape wasn't loved by everyone. Nevertheless, despite the detractors, the TR7 went on to become the best-selling TR of them all.

Triumph TR8 – 1979-1981

Triumph belatedly squeezed a 3528cc Rover V8 under the sloping bonnet of the TR7 in 1979. Had there been such an option from the start, gifting the car with 137bhp and a 120mph capability, it might have saved the model range but, instead, the TR8 had a very limited production life. Most of the 2722 built headed to the United States; hardly any remained in the UK. However, the TR8 gave a glimpse of what the TR7 could have been – meaning that enthusiasts have been converting their own TR7s ever since.

TVR 2500M/3000M – 1972-1977

During the 1960s and 1970s, TVR styling evolved very slowly; an early-1970s car looked much the same as one from a decade earlier, bar a few nips and tucks. It was under the surface that the mechanical magic happened. The M-Series cars came along in 1972, with a stuffer backbone, all-independent suspension and longer body. The 2500M had a 2498cc TR6 engine, aimed at the USA where it could meet tough environmental rules. There were fewer concerns in Britain at the time, so the 3000M had a Ford Capri 2994cc V6 and easily out-paced its smaller-engined sister.

Vauxhall Firenza Droopsnoot – 1973-1975

There was the Firenza, and then there was the Firenza Droopsnoot. The Firenza was Vauxhall's attempt to 'do a Capri' with the Viva HC, with a fastback coupe rear replacing the duller saloon tail. The Droopsnoot went even further. It was only available with the biggest 2279cc engine, the twin cams and 131 brake horses which allowed a top speed of 120mph. However, what really got it noticed was the glassfibre nose cone, boot spoiler and special wheels. Inexplicably, just 204 were sold.

Vauxhall Chevette 2300HS – 1976-1979

The HS was a homologation special, built so that Vauxhall could go rallying with its family Chevette. The 2279cc engine was the same as in the Firenza Droopsnoot, and there were front and rear spoilers and alloy wheels to further distinguish this RS Escort-beater from the herd. A further evolution was the HSR, but it was intended for the rally track rather than the road. 400 HSs were made, along with 50 HSRs.

Chapter 8

Charging Through the 1980s

Turbocharging, hot hatches and wave after wave of foreign imports meant that British sports car builders had a lot to contend with during the 1980s.

The era of the traditional open sports car seemed over by the 1980s. Cars like the MGB, MG Midget, Triumph Spitfire and TR7 just about survived to greet the decade, but then promptly vanished. The marques that built them were also killed off by British Leyland, to the sadness of many. Triumph disappeared completely in 1984 after a short spell building the Acclaim, a badge-engineered Honda Ballade that was anything but sporting. MG wasn't completely dispensed with but became just a brand for 'breathed on' Austin Metros, Montegos and Maestros.

Such 'hot hatches' were the new vogue. The trend had started during the 1970s but gathered even more pace during the 1980s, spearheaded by models such as the Volkswagen Golf GTI and Peugeot 205 GTI. These small, but very usable, high-performance versions of everyday family runarounds quickly took the place of the older sports cars. Britain lagged behind its continental European counterparts in building hot hatches, having relied for too long on ageing models despite all the signs that their time was up. It was only during the 1980s that UK manufacturers fully joined the hot hatch revolution, although by then, rivals from abroad had the upper hand. Ford, however, would belatedly produce some of the best hot hatches of the period.

Another new phenomenon that flourished during the decade was turbocharging. During the 1970s, forced induction was generally something only found on the most exotic sports cars. Then, the Swedish manufacturer Saab brought it more into the mainstream on models such as its 99 and 900. Before long, turbocharging became practically vital for manufacturers seeking to boost performance without wanting to go to the trouble of increasing cubic capacity. Nor was it enough just to fit a turbocharger – or twin turbochargers – and keep it discreet. The decade's love of labels saw many models reference turbocharging in their names – step forward Bentley, Lotus and MG among others – while the obligatory flashy graphics were a way of making sure that everybody else knew your engine had something extra bolted on.

All this was happening against a backdrop of increasing imports into Britain. These weren't just from over the other side of the English Channel. Japanese autos, little more than a trickle during the 1970s, became a wave in the 1980s. While family cars were the mainstay of the invasion, there were high-performance machines as well. British dealerships and streets were now becoming very crowded with foreign rivals, and homegrown manufacturers were having to up their game to compete.

Aston Martin Virage – 1989-2000

The curvaceous V8 had served Aston Martin well since the early 1970s, but towards the end of the 1980s, it became clear that it needed a successor, with so many more modern rivals crowding the field. Aston's response was the Virage; a very imposing and purposeful new shape that neatly masked the continuing use of the old V8 chassis underneath, with the V8 engine upgraded to 32 valves. 330bhp was the usual state of tune, but in later Vantage versions, 550bhp and 600bhp was the order of the day thanks to the benefits of twin supercharging.

Bentley Turbo R – 1985-1992

Bentley had been in the long shadow of its parent company Rolls-Royce since the 1950s, but the 1980s finally marked the start of its revival as a performance marque. The Bentley Turbo R may have been based on the Rolls-Royce Silver Spirit, but it was a very different beast thanks to the turbocharged 6750cc V8 engine that, with 328bhp, was around 50 per cent more powerful than that of its Spirit of Ecstasy sister. The 'R' in the name stood for roadholding, to indicate that there had been attention to the suspension as well.

Bristol Brigand – 1982-1994

More turbocharging, this time in something that probably didn't really need it in the first place. The Britannia already had a 335bhp Chrysler 5898cc V8, but Bristol still saw fit to install a turbocharger and rename the boosted car the Brigand. Actual power was never disclosed, but it seems that at least 20 per cent more power was added. What was known was that the Brigand could achieve 150mph, hitting 60mph on the way there in just 5.9 seconds.

Ford Capri 280 Brooklands – 1987

The final version of the Capri was undoubtedly the best. The limited edition Capri 280, with 160bhp, 2792cc V6 power, featured Brooklands Green metallic paint – hence their 'Brooklands' nickname – plus special 15-inch alloy wheels and full leather inside. They were very good-looking cars, capable of almost 130mph, that saw out the Ford's most popular sports coupe in real style. There was no direct replacement for the Capri because hot hatches were by now ruling the roads.

Ford Escort XR3/XR3i – 1981-1986

One of Ford's most popular hot hatches, the 1.6-litre XR3 started out in 1981 with a carburettor and 96bhp but then got fuel injection and 105bhp in 1983. Fun rather than fabulously fast, it was nevertheless capable of116mph, while looking just as a performance saloon should have done during the Eighties, with distinctive alloy wheels and black trim. A 'boy racer' favourite.

Ford Sierra RS Cosworth – 1985-1987

One of the high-performance monsters of the 1980s, the Ford Sierra Cosworth was loud, proud and proof of just how capable the Sierra was. A turbocharged 204bhp Cosworth 1993cc engine allowed speeds of up to 145mph, or 149mph with the more highly tuned 224bhp RS500. But the 'Cossie was almost as much about posing as it was going quickly; that huge rear spoiler made it patently clear that this was not a Ford to be messed with.

Ford RS200 – 1984-1986

The mid-engined Ford RS200 was primarily a Group B rally car, but some 200 examples had to be built for the road for homologation purposes. Cosworth did the tricksy stuff on the turbocharged 1803cc engine, while FF Developments was responsible for the four-wheel drive. States of tune ranged from a 'mild' 250bhp up to an extremely wild 650bhp.

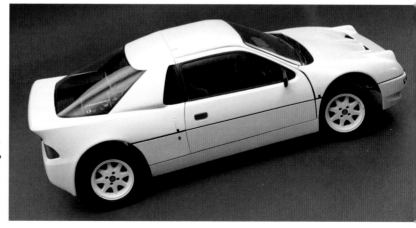

Lotus Excel – 1982-1992

The Excel was based on the earlier Eclat, with revisions made to the body. However, most of the changes were mechanical, with transmissions, brakes and some suspension parts now courtesy of Toyota. A galvanised chassis meant that even the bits that weren't glassfibre were now rust-resistant. The 180bhp SE of 1986 was the stand-out variant.

Lotus Esprit Turbo – 1980-1987

The Esprit always had supercar looks, but its performance had fallen somewhat short of that territory. The Esprit Turbo changed that, adding an extra 50bhp to the reworked 2174cc engine. There was also an aerodynamic bodykit. The first 45 wore a rather lurid Essex Overseas Petroleum Corporation livery, which was sponsoring Team Lotus at the time, but later examples toned down the graphics. With the Esprit Turbo, Lotus had a car that was fast enough to fully exploit the already superb handling.

Lotus Esprit X180 – 1987-1994

By the mid-1980s, the origami folded lines of the original Giugiaro-penned Esprit were looking a little too hard-edged. So the Esprit was 'restyled' by British designer Peter Stevens, who managed to add some curves while still keeping the Lotus close to its original look. It was a subtle but effective refresh that gave the car a new lease of life.

Lotus Elan M100 – 1989-1994

Lotus revived the old Elan name for its opening foray into front-wheel drive. It seemed suitable, given that the new holder of the title was an attractive compact roadster that, like its ancestor, could outmanoeuvre anything else around. Isuzu 1588cc engines, in both turbocharged and normally aspirated forms, provided the power. Sadly, the M100 Elan didn't do nearly as well as its earlier namesake; only 4655 were sold.

MG Metro Turbo – 1983-1989

With the closure of MG's Abingdon factory and the end of its sports cars, it seemed like the end for MG at the dawn of the 1980s. However, to give British Leyland its due, it recognised that the marque's name still stood for a lot, and soon reintroduced it on badge-engineered, souped-up Metros. The standard 1275cc MG Metro only had an extra 12bhp compared to its Austin equivalent, but Lotus was brought in for the Turbo variant. It managed to extract 93bhp in total and turned the little Metro, then one of Britain's most popular family cars, into a neat little hot hatch. But more was to follow...

MG Maestro Turbo – 1989-1991

If the MG Metro Turbo was fun, its bigger MG Maestro Turbo sister was really quite serious. The Montego Turbo's 152bhp 1994cc engine found itself transported under the bonnet of the smaller MG Maestro, suitably decorated with a bodykit and Turbo graphics. With the claimed capability of zero to 60mph in just 6.7 seconds, it was advertised as being faster than a Ferrari, Porsche, Lamborghini, Lotus, Aston Martin... which must have been very upsetting for owners of all those cars.

Middlebridge Scimitar GTE – 1988-1990

Reliant's Scimitar GTE was the sports estate that wouldn't die. The rights to the car were bought by Middlebridge in 1987, which planned to hand-build them at a rate of 300 per year. Upgrades included a more mighty 2933cc V6 Ford engine plus suspension tweaks to improve the handling. Inside, there was greater luxury as well. However, the price tag of £24,000 – substantially more than the older but less well-specced Reliant version – meant that a mere 77 appeared. Princess Anne was a fan.

Panther Solo – 1989-1990

The Panther Solo was a fascinating what-might-have-been car. After all the company's retro-styled cars, the Solo was a futuristic sports coupe with such novel features as aluminium honeycomb, composites and carbon-fibre construction, revolving hidden headlamps and four-wheel drive. Powering the car was a Ford Sierra RS 1993cc engine of 204bhp. It was an eye-catching creation in 1989, but also an expensive one. Even though Panther said it was only going to make 100 in total, it struggled to turn out under a quarter of those.

Reliant Scimitar SS1 – 1984-1989

With the MGB and Triumph TR7 dropped, Reliant figured it could fill the void with a small, cheap, wedge-shaped roadster. Actually, the Scimitar SS1 did offer decent handling and performance from its variety of sub-two-litre Ford engines, and all at a very acceptable price. But where it fell down was in its awkward, layered styling, which was started by master Italian designer Giovanni Michelotti, but never completed, as he died before he could do so. With better looks, it could have done very well.

TVR Tasmin – 1980-1984

After decades of voluptuous curves, TVR went wedgy in 1980 with the Tasmin. Despite the up-to-date appearance – which would unfortunately date quite quickly, as other cars were already going back to more rounded lines after the square-cut 1970s – the chassis and mechanics of earlier cars were carried over, as they already did their job very well. Among the engine options for the Tasmin were a Ford 1993cc four-cylinder unit, the trusted and effective 2792cc V6 from the same company and, eventually, Rover's ubiquitous 3528cc V8.

TVR 450SEAC – 1988-1989

The ultimate genesis of the Tasmin saw it christened the 450SEAC, with a greatly enlarged 4441cc version of Rover's V8. Combined with a lightweight shell – the SEAC of the title standing for 'Special Equipment Aramid Composite' to denote the carbon-fibre and Kevlar used – the 450SEAC was the fastest TVR to date. It didn't run out of steam until it reached 155mph and could get there faster than a Lamborghini Countach.

Vauxhall Astra MkII GTE 16V – 1988-1991

Partly thanks to its effective aerodynamics, the Vauxhall Astra GTE 16V was one of the fastest mainstream hot hatches of the Eighties. A very creditable 156bhp was extracted from its 1998cc double overhead-cam engine, making it feel a world away from the family Astras it was based on. None of them could come close to the GTE 16V's 134mph maximum. It could be a bit of a handful to keep on the straight and narrow, though. Inside, the digital dash made drivers feel like even a trip to Tesco's was a *Knight Rider* adventure.

Vauxhall Lotus Carlton – 1990-1992

One of the bad boys of the 1980s, the Lotus Carlton was a supercar in saloon form. Its 3615cc six-cylinder 377bhp engine could catapult it to 175mph, with 60mph taking just 4.8 seconds from rest. Yet it did all this looking largely the same as the Carltons that people were buying as family transport. Both the *Daily Mail* and Association of Chief Police Officers wanted it banned because it was just too fast. But that would have upset the thieves and joyriders who so loved it, and the awe-struck owners who loved it even more.

Chapter 9

Scaling Back in the 1990s

Small seemed beautiful again in the 1990s, and brands like MG, TVR and even Vauxhall made the most of being able to sell to new customers. It was no longer all about hatchbacks.

The hot hatches that had dominated the previous decade were all very well, but they couldn't quite equal the raw appeal of true sports cars. That is why, after falling out of fashion in the 1980s, proper roadsters returned with a vengeance in the 1990s. It was the popularity of the Mazda MX-5, which hearkened back to the sporty small machines of the Sixties, that kick-started interest in the real things again, especially if it came in convertible form, and was rather rapid too. The MX-5's success prompted cars like the MGF, led indirectly to Vauxhall's VX220 and helped to ignite interest in TVR's new models. The chance to enjoy small, open, fast machines again was something very welcome.

There was room for bigger toys, too. Aston Martin launched its most successful model ever, the DB7, and Bentley started returning to its performance roots. Jaguar's sports cars included the awesome XJ220 and XK8, while McLaren's F1 exceeded even supercar expectations. If there was one thing certain about the 1990s, it was that nothing was predictable – it was a decade of anything goes.

Aston Martin DB7 – 1993-2004

Ford took over Aston Martin in 1988, and the access to the Blue Oval's considerable resources paid dividends for the British specialist manufacturer. It was able to launch the beautiful DB7 in 1993, as probably the most accessible Aston ever. The new car shared a lot of its make-up with Jaguar – also part of the Ford family at the time – and turned its back on the V8 engines that had been around for the last 20 years in favour of a supercharged 335bhp, 3228cc straight-six. This (almost) affordable Aston sold in greater numbers than any of the marque's previous models. This pushed Ford to launch a 5935cc V12 version in 1999, which did even better.

Bentley Continental R – 1991-2003

A big step in Bentley's revival was 1991's Bentley Continental R. Recalling a great Bentley model of the past with its name, the Continental also got its own individualistic styling, which wasn't shared with any Rolls-Royce – at least from the waist up. The streamlined coupe style and 152mph top speed were a reminder that Bentley had once been one of the great sporting brands, and could be again.

Caterham 21 – 1996-1999

Caterham's 21st birthday present to itself was an attempt to update the venerable, raw Seven into a more practical and stylish machine, with streamlined, modern bodywork masking the existing chassis. The Rover K-Series engines ranged from 113bhp to 190bhp. This grown-up Caterham was a more civilised experience than the Seven. Then, of all companies, Lotus launched the Elise and stole the 21's thunder. Just 49 were made up until 1999, against projections of 250 per year.

Ford Escort RS Cosworth – 1992-1996

Another of Ford's flamboyant but very competent hot hatches, the RS Cosworth was based on a shortened Sierra Cosworth 4x4 platform. The reasoning behind it was that Ford needed a rally car, but between 1992 and 1996, over 7,000 were sold as road cars. The rear spoiler was huge (and like a red rag to other bulls on the road), but with 227bhp and a turbocharger, it was probably very advisable to help keep within the limits of this RS on the Tarmac.

Jaguar XJ220 – 1992-1994

The XJ220 was Jaguar letting its wildest ambitions run wild; a monstrous, four-wheel-drive, mid-V12-engined sinuous supercar that was utterly unlike vehicles it had come up with before. 1,500 orders were taken when it was revealed at the 1988 Motor Show in Birmingham, but by the time the production version appeared in 1991, its V12 had been replaced by the MG Metro rally car's 6R4 turbocharged V6 instead, and it was rear-wheel-drive only. This, and the early 1990s recession, meant that orders for the £470,000 200mph-plus hypermachine collapsed, and only 271 were produced.

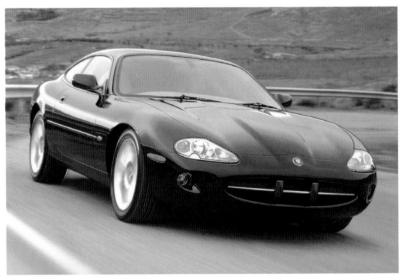

Jaguar XK8/XKR – 1996-2005

The lovely XK8 superseded the XJS in 1996, and it wasn't a moment too soon. It felt like Jaguar had a proper sports car in its armoury again, even if the chassis of the XJS was retained. However, the 290bhp, 3996cc V8 engine was fresh off the shelf and was enough to do the sprint to 60mph in under 6.6 seconds. The top speed had to be limited to 155mph. The XKR of 1998 just made everything better still, by using a supercharger to add a very handy extra 80bhp.

Lotus Esprit V8 – 1996-2004

The Esprit was magnificent enough with its four-cylinder engine, whether turbocharged or not. However, in 1996, room was found to squeeze Lotus' own 3506cc V8 engine into the (near) centre of it, as well as to fit two turbochargers, to give 350bhp. The Esprit was a genuine supercar now, with a maximum velocity of 175mph for anybody with enough road and bravery to try and achieve it.

Lotus Elise – 1996-2021

The Elise was Lotus returning to what it had always done best; a small, featherweight, rear-wheel drive open sports car that didn't need oodles of power to deliver the goods. The first Elises had Rover K-Series engines that delivered between 118bhp and 158bhp, but there was so little weight that 126mph was still possible. However, Lotuses have never been about outright speed. Amazing handling has always been more significant, and the Elise was up there with the very best.

McLaren F1 – 1993-1997

McLaren's F1 was nothing less than a no-compromises hypercar, intended to show the world what the motorsport firm was capable of even away from the racetrack. Its slippery shape housed a specially built 6064cc BMW V12 engine, mid-mounted naturally, which put out a phenomenal 627bhp. What could it do with that? About 240mph and nought to 60mph in just 3.2 seconds, while seating three people, with the driver in the centre of the seating row. There was just nothing like it at the time, and there has been very little like it since. It was a staggering British sports car and a landmark in the history of the breed.

MG RV8 – 1992-1995

The MGB had been a best-seller and was still much-loved in the 1990s as a classic. Why not revive it? MG's custodian, Rover, did just that mid-decade, using new bodyshells combined with 3947cc Range Rover V8 engines. While only 1,983 of these 135mph reborn roadsters were made, it helped to convince Rover that there was now a market again for proper MG sports cars.

MGF – 1995-2001

Enthusiasts were delighted when MG returned to true sports cars again with the MGF – and it turned out to be pretty great, too. There was some surprise that it was mid-engined, but that gave it an air of sophistication as well as excellent road manners. The Hydragas (fluid and gas) suspension was also unusual for a sports car, but it worked remarkably well and gave a more compliant ride than was usual with small, budget sports cars. Sealing the deal on the new MG was the pretty two-seater body, while the K-Series engines – of 118bhp and 143bhp – delivered peppy performance. The TF replaced it in 2002, with similar looks but a more conventional suspension.

Rover 220 Coupe – 1992-1998

Rover's 220 Coupe was a surprisingly attractive adaptation of the existing saloon, with a lowered, fastback roofline. It also had the muscle to back up its looks; a turbocharged 1994cc engine of 197bhp delivering a top speed that came achingly close to 150mph. It was remarkable for a Rover. The nickname of 'Tomcat' – a reference to its project code name – seemed a very apt, given its boisterous but entertaining character.

Rover 200 BRM – 1998

Rover traded on its long-past relationship with Formula One team British Racing Motors (BRM) for the limited edition 200 BRM in 1998. It was an interesting, limited-edition sports model that took several styling cues from BRM racers, such as the British Racing Green paint and orange air intake up front. Inside, there was a LOT of quilted red leather. This all made it something of an oddity at the time, and one which took a long time to sell out its 1,100 production run, but there is a hardcore cult following today.

TVR Griffith – 1991-2002

The Griffith was a return to curves for TVR, and its design was a particularly gorgeous and uncluttered piece of work; a classically good-looking sports car. The various V8 engines meant that this TVR lived up to the promise of its appearance. The real importance of the Griffith is that it dragged customers back to TVR in droves, signalling a revival of interest in the Blackpool specialist manufacturer.

TVR Chimaera – 1993-2003

The Chimaera was closely related to the Griffith but had slightly larger dimensions, making it more of a grand tourer rather than an outright sports cars. Because it used the same chassis plus V8 engines, it offered much the same experience. There is an urban legend that the design of the sidelights came about because company owner Peter Wheeler's dog took a bite out of the clay model, and he liked the result so much that he decided to keep it.

TVR Cerbera – 1996-2003

TVR had been using other people's engines since it started, but that changed with the Cerbera. The 3996cc, 4185cc and 4475cc V8 engines, of 360bhp and 420bhp, respectively, had teething troubles, but when they were working as they should, they allowed speeds in excess of 170mph – with the 4.5-litre V8 making 185mph attainable in the right circumstances. Offering a roof plus 2+2 seating made the Cerbera the model for those who liked their TVRs a little more well-done than raw.

TVR Tuscan Speed Six – 1999-2006

It was back to the historic Tuscan name for one of the most radial-looking TVRs, with its cascading, wave-like lines and stacked headlamps. Even for TVR, it was an astonishing machine which it was impossible not to stare at – especially in one of the trick paint schemes. 3605cc and 3996cc V8s meant this crazy concoction, with a removable roof panel and rear window, delivered the sporting goods just as effortlessly as its several sisters did.

Vauxhall VX220 – 1999-2005

Although sold as both a Vauxhall and an Opel, the VX220 was really a Lotus – it was built by the company in Norfolk and was a reworked version of the Lotus Elise. The money from General Motors (which owned Opel and Vauxhall), allowed Lotus to develop the Elise and, in return, GM's European arms got a mid-engined, two-seater sports car. For the VX220, there were bigger two-litre and 2.2-litre GM engines, a new body was fitted (still glassfibre, as on the Elise) and the interior was made a bit plusher, with additional safety features. Even so, it still seemed something very left-of-centre from Vauxhall.

Chapter 10

New Directions for a New Century

The sports cars of the 21st Century are faster, sleeker, sexier and more complex than ever before. But environmental concerns and relentless technological progress mean their days could well be numbered.

The 21st Century has brought new challenges for sports car manufacturers. Electronics have played an increasingly important role in cars since the 1980s, but our current, connected age has just accelerated the process. Even the cheapest, most mainstream cars are packed with hi-tech and for those building high-performance machines, the need to be ahead of the curve is paramount. Computers control every single aspect of a modern vehicle. It is no longer just enough to build a car that is mechanically advanced and well-engineered; a modern sports car needs electronics that can alter and adapt its characteristics to conditions in a micro-second. Building a decent sports car never used to be rocket science, but it might as well be now.

The current crop of sports cars probably represents the last hurrah for the internal combustion engine. While many of the cars in this chapter deliver exhilaration and competence beyond anything possible in the 20th Century, they are likely to be the last of their breed. Sales of new petrol cars will be banned in Britain from 2030, with even hybrid ones only granted a stay of execution until 2035. Consequently, the market for electric vehicles is growing rapidly. Jaguar has announced that it will become an all-electric car brand from 2025, while Aston Martin also intends to replace its current DB11 with a fully electric model that year. Lotus unveiled its first series production electric sports car, the Evija, in July 2019, billing it as the first all-British, all-electric hypercar, with speeds of over 200mph and a range of 215 miles. The need to build machines with alternative powertrains capable of both speed and distance is a problem facing all car makers, but it is an especially acute issue for sports car producers. While electric motors offer acceleration and velocities well beyond most petrol engines, high speed saps power quickly. Balancing these factors will be one of the keys to building the great sports cars of the future.

There are some who question whether there is even a future for sports car while SUVs – some of them very rapid – and autonomous vehicles are proliferating. But, thankfully, a world where we all potter around in self-driving pods still seems quite a long way ahead. Until then, just as in the very first days of the car, there is always going to be somebody who wants to go just that little faster than everybody else, and to do so in a stylish way, too…

Ariel Atom – 2000-present

What started out in the mid-1990s as a Coventry University student project is now one of the rawest, most eye-catching and utterly exhilarating sports cars ever. The Atom is about as close to a racing car for the road as it is possible to get – in fact, it is hard to believe the model is road legal, but it is. Creature comforts are pretty much non-existent. There are no doors, windows or roof, and the lightweight chassis is exposed with hardly any panelling. But the Atom isn't about pampering. It's about going very, very fast. There have been eight generations of Atom to date, with power outputs ranging from 190bhp to 500bhp, the latter with a three-litre V8 and a claimed zero to 60mph time of under 2.3 seconds. Utterly mad, but in a good way.

Aston Martin V12 Vanquish – 2001-2007

After the success of the DB7 and its 1999 upgrade with a 5935cc V12 engine, Aston Martin pushed ahead with a new flagship model, the Vanquish. It came with a bonded aluminium composite chassis with carbon fibre backbone and, naturally, the V12 engine but in more potent state of tune than the DB7 – 460bhp compared to 420bhp. Still, for some, 190mph and nought to 60mph in 4.5 seconds just wasn't rapid enough, so by 2004 there was the Vanquish S with 520bhp and a 200mph capability. Pierce Brosnan's James Bond inexplicably had an 'invisible' Vanquish in *Die Another Day*, but that was about the only time people felt let down by a Vanquish.

Aston Martin DB9 – 2004-2016

The successor to the DB7 featured all-aluminium construction and used the V12 engine of the Vanquish – a model it quite closely resembled – tuned to produce 450bhp. However, Aston Martin could never be content to just let that lie, and for 2009, there was a hike to 470bhp followed by 510bhp in 2013. Whatever variant you went for, the car could come close to 200mph while still looking as elegantly British as a Savile Row suit.

Aston Martin Vantage – 2005-2018

The 2005 Vantage, as Aston Martin's smallest model, was focused more on outright agility, in order to pitch it against cars like the Porsche 911. It also brought a V8 back to the Aston line-up, initially in 380bhp 4280cc form and then, from 2008, a 420bhp 4735cc. This was mounted well back in the chassis to give excellent weight distribution and thus exemplary handling. There were also V12 variants, the 565bhp option transforming the Vantage S into a 205mph projectile. An all-new Vantage was introduced in 2018, with its spectacular looks inspired by the DB10 used in Bond film *Spectre*.

Aston Martin DB11 – 2016-present

The replacement for the DB9 skipped the DB10 designation, because that was reserved solely for the bespoke cars created for the 2015 *Spectre* 007 movie. There was a new adhesive-bonded aluminium platform and a fresh 5204cc V12. This may have been smaller in capacity than the V12 of its forebears but, thanks to twin turbochargers, achieved 600bhp. Aston's tie up with Mercedes-Benz led to an 'entry level' V8 503bhp variant in 2017. Both the V12 and the V8 have received recent power upgrades.

Bentley Continental GT – 2003-present

Thanks to Volkswagen's ownership of Bentley, this was practically a mass-produced Bentley compared to previous models. It returned the marque closer to its sporting roots, as a proper – if large – GT that wasn't based on a Rolls-Royce model. What lay beneath the Bentley's beautiful body was based on the Volkswagen Phaeton limo and employed a 5998cc W12 engine with four-wheel drive to propel this big boy to 200mph. There have now been three generations of Continental GT and it is a mark of how spot-on the original design was that it still retains the same basic shape today.

Jaguar F-type – 2013-present

At long last, a proper successor to the E-type. The 2013 introduction of the F-type gave Jaguar a true sports machine, and one that was deemed worthy of continuing the lineage of the immortal E. Supercharged three-litre V6s and five-litre V8s were the original engine options, with the latter allowing 200mph to be reached in its most extreme 567bhp SVR form.

Lotus Exige – 2000-2021

The Exige took the Elise roadster as its starting point but added a roof and other styling enhancements, plus more poke to the mid-mounted 1796cc Rover K-Series engine. As expected of a Lotus, lightness was paramount, so the 177bhp and 192bhp options were more than adequate for a 136mph top speed and sub-five second sprint to 60mph. The Series II of 2004 switched to an even more energetic Toyota engine, while 2013's Series III went above and beyond with a 3456cc V6. For those talented enough to try it, up to 180mph was possible, but this car was more about the cornering than the outright speed.

Lotus Evora – 2009-2021

Lotus had focused on small sports cars during the opening years of the 21st Century, but the Evora was a larger and more practical machine – you could fit a pair of golf clubs in the boot behind the mid-mounted Toyota 3456cc V6 here, as well as two people in the back seats. Although it was still a squeeze...

McLaren MP4-12C – 2011-2014

The MP4-12C title was hardly evocative – it sounded more like something you would call a photocopier – but with a twin-turbocharged, mid-mounted 3799cc V8 engine, this McLaren was far more exciting than any office equipment. There was nothing remotely bland about the 218mph potential and zero to 60mph time of 2.8 seconds, plus deployment of Formula One technology on a road car. By the end of 2012, even McLaren realised the moniker was far too cumbersome and the model became known just as the 12C in coupe form, with the convertible rechristened the 12C Spider.

McLaren 570S – 2015-present

A practical McLaren? That was the thinking behind the 570S, with greater 'day-to-day usability and driveability' dialled in than was usually found on the company's single-minded performance machines. While there may have been more luggage and interior space, plus greater luxury, this was hardly a Volvo estate, so was still capable of over 200mph and getting to 60mph from rest in 3.2 seconds.

MINI Cooper S – 2000-present

Just as with the classic Mini, BMW's new 21st-century MINI has its own racy variant in the form of the Mini Cooper S. With the original 2000-2006 R53 incarnation, this meant a supercharged 1598cc engine, styling cues that echoed the earlier 20th Century cars, and a huge amount of driving fun. The Cooper S certainly had swiftness and sure-footedness on its side. The model has continued throughout subsequent generations of the MINI, but enthusiasts appreciate the simplicity and purity of the R53.

Morgan Aero 8 – 2000-2018

The new Morgan of 2000 was something radical for a company not known for styling progress. While there was a modernised resemblance to its siblings that still made it unmistakeably a Morgan, the 4398cc BMW V8 meant it could go way beyond any previous model – to over 160mph, in fact. The main talking point on early cars was the cross-eyed appearance, thanks to the use of Volkswagen Beetle headlamps but, in 2005, MINI headlights corrected the focus. In AeroMax coupe form this Morgan for a new century was particularly striking.

Noble M600 – 2010-present

Noble Automotive may only have been founded in 1999, but it has forged quite a reputation for itself, thanks to products like the M600. With three bodies – two coupes, one with a glassfibre body, the other a carbon-fibre one, and a Speedster with removable roof panels – the M600 has epic specifications thanks to its 4414cc Volvo (yes, Volvo!) V8. The nought to 60mph time of three seconds is impressive enough, but the M600 can reach 200mph in under half a minute and still have something in reserve.